THE CATHOLIC UNIVERSITY OF AMERICA
CANON LAW STUDIES
No. 262

CENSORSHIP OF SPECIAL CLASSES OF BOOKS

(Canons 1387–1391)

A HISTORY AND COMMENTARY

BY

NATHANIEL L. SONNTAG, O.F.M.Cap., J.C.L.
OF THE PROVINCE OF ST. JOSEPH

A DISSERTATION
SUBMITTED TO THE FACULTY OF THE SCHOOL OF CANON LAW
OF THE CATHOLIC UNIVERSITY OF AMERICA IN PARTIAL
FULFILLMENT OF THE REQUIREMENTS FOR THE
DEGREE OF DOCTOR OF CANON LAW

THE CATHOLIC UNIVERSITY OF AMERICA PRESS
WASHINGTON, D. C.
1947

Imprimi Potest:
EDMUNDUS J. KRAMER, O.F.M.Cap.,
Minister Provincialis
Detroiti, die 2 iunii, 1947

Nihil Obstat:
EDUARDUS G. ROELKER, S.T.D., J.C.D.,
Censor Deputatus,
Washingtonii, D. C., die 31 maii, 1947

Imprimatur:
✠ JOANNES M. McNAMARA, D.D.,
Vicarius Capitularis Baltimorensis-Washingtoniensis
Baltimorae, die 2 iunii, 1947

MURRAY & HEISTER—WASHINGTON, D. C.
PRINTED IN THE UNITED STATES OF AMERICA

9

To My
Mother and My Father

TABLE OF CONTENTS

CHAPTER IV

LITURGICAL BOOKS AND LITANIES (Canon 1390)

CHAPTER V

TRANSLATIONS OF THE SACRED SCRIPTURES (Canon 1391)

FOREWORD

Censorship of Special Classes of Books, a history and commentary on canons 1387–1391, presupposes a knowledge of the general norms of censorship enacted in canons 1384–1386 and 1392–1394. In particular, it takes for granted an acquaintance with the basic terminology, e.g., book, booklet, pamphlet, leaflet, author, editor, compiler, printer, publisher, edition, publication, reprint, censorship, permission, approval, prohibition, etc.

The censorship of books received wide attention and elaborate discussion at the turn of the century, shortly after Pope Leo XIII (1878–1903) issued his Constitution "*Officiorum ac munerum,*" January 25, 1897. Since the close of the first decade of the present century, censorship has been quite neglected, save for the usual condensed references in commentaries, manuals and compendia. No books have been written on it; extremely few articles discussed it in periodicals. This study, then, is an attempt to restore this practical subject to the attention it deserves.

Not all the canons on censorship are treated in this dissertation. The five canons treated here have an independent history and an independent commentary; and, as such, form an independent unit.

The writer expresses his gratitude to his Superiors in the Capuchin Order for the opportunity to pursue advanced studies in Canon Law, particularly to the Most Rev. Clement Neubauer, O.F.M.Cap., Minister General, and to the Very Rev. Edmund Kramer, O.F.M.Cap., Minister Provincial; to the Capuchin Friars of the Province of St. Augustine for their kindness and hospitality during his residence at Capuchin College, Brookland, D. C.; to the Faculty of the School of Canon Law at The Catholic University of America, Washington, D. C., for their guidance and assistance; to the Rev. Donald Wiest, O.F.M.Cap., J.C.L., for valuable assistance in research; and to all others who have aided in any way in the preparation of this work.

CHAPTER I

PROCESSES OF BEATIFICATION AND CANONIZATION

(Canon 1387)

Quae ad causas beatificationum et canonizationum Servorum Dei quoquo modo pertinent, sine licentia Sacrorum Rituum Congregationis edi nequeunt.

At first glance one might be led to believe that canon 1387 includes all material pertaining to the Servants of God which may have some bearing on their beatification or canonization. A closer reading of the canon, however, indicates that its only concern is the process of beatification and canonization. The history of the canon, as well as the commentary, confirms the restricted view as the only correct interpretation.

A. History

The history of canon 1387 will treat of: (1) an early institute in the Church known as the Acts of the Martyrs; (2) the actual development of the legislation referring to the publication of the processes of beatification and canonization.

(1) Acts of the Martyrs

The Acts of the Martyrs (*Acta Martyrum*) are documents in the form of official records kept by the notaries of the Roman Courts during the trial, sentence, punishment and death of the early Christian martyrs.[1] As soon as the Church was able to gain access to these authentic records she allowed them to be read in the churches, obviously for the edification of the faithful.[2]

[1] Dufourcq, *Études sur les Gesta Martyrum Romains* (Paris, 1900), pp. 265–269.

[2] Thus, for instance, the III Council of Carthage (398): "Item placuit,

Often such official acts were not available. Private persons, with the best of intentions, began to write and publish their own accounts of the martyrs in the form of acts. These substitutes were acceptable as long as the narrator was an eyewitness; or, at least, as long as he sifted the evidence carefully. The Church made every attempt to keep these acts reliable. During the persecutions, however, many documents perished. Under Diocletian (284–305), in particular, many were purposely destroyed. Oral tradition preserved the stories of the more famous martyrs until they were rewritten,[3] but it is all too easy to see how deterioration of the records could set in. There was altogether too much latitude for introducing legends. Spurious acts were also manufactured. Hence, a Council held at Rome (494) condemned the reading of all Acts of the Martyrs in church.[4] Gradually the public reading of the acts in church fell into desuetude. And although these documents were originally official in character, the Church never considered them as part of her own system of giving public honor to a martyr.

The decision to give public honors to a martyr rested with the bishop of the place where the person died. Those martyrs whose holiness had been confirmed by a bishop were known as proved (*vindicati*) martyrs. Only the Bishop of Rome could extend the permission for the public veneration of martyrs to all the churches, for he alone had authority over all.[5] Pope Alexander III (1159–1181) restricted the use of the process of beatification of a Servant of God to the Holy See,[6] at least when a particular case was involved. It is not clear whether the Pope intended to restrict this as an exclusive power to the Holy See. Bishops continued

---

ut praeter scripturas canonicas nihil in ecclesia legatur . . . liceat autem legi passiones martyrum cum anniversarii dies eorum celebrantur"—Mansi, *Sacrorum Conciliorum Nova et Amplissima Collectio* (53 vols. in 60, Florentiae, Parisiis, Arnhem, et Leipzig, 1901–1927), III, 892 (hereafter cited as Mansi).

[3] This explains why the earliest extant copies of the acts date from the sixth century. Cf. Dufourcq, *Études*, pp. 27–293.

[4] Migne, *Patrologiae Cursus Completus, Series Latina* (221 vols., Parisiis, 1844–1864), LIX, 171–172.

[5] Duchesne, *Origines du culte chrétien* (5. ed., Paris, 1925), p. 284.

[6] C. 1, X, *de reliquiis et veneratione sanctorum,* III, 45.

to take cognizance of the causes of saintly persons, proceeding even as far as beatification.

(2) DEVELOPMENT OF THE LAW ENACTED IN CANON 1387

The election of Pope Urban VIII (1623–1644) to the throne of Peter marked the advent of a new era in the law concerning the veneration of the Servants of God. Throughout his long pontificate Urban treated this subject again and again. His enactments form a starting point from which stems a double series of decrees —one concerning the printing of the lives, deeds, virtues, miracles, etc., of the Servants of God, and the other concerning the printing of the processual acts of beatification and canonization.

(a) *Printing of the Lives, etc., of the Servants of God*

1. Legislation of Urban VIII (1623–1644)

Among Urban's earliest decrees there is one which contains a paragraph that is of interest here:

> Ac pariter imprimi de caetero inhibuit libros eorundem hominum, qui Sanctitatis, sive Martyrii fama, vel opinione, ut praefertur, celebres e vita migraverint, gesta miracula, vel revelationes, seu quaecumque beneficia tamquam eorum intercessionibus a Deo accepta continentes, sine recognitione, atque approbatione Ordinarii, qui in iis recognoscendis Theologos, aliosque pios, ac doctos viros in consilium adhibeat, et ne deinceps fraus, aut error, aut aliquid novum, ac inordinatum in re tam gravi committatur, negotium instructum ad Sedem Apostolicam transmittat, eiusque responsum expectet. Revelationes vero, et miracula, aliaque beneficia supradicta, quae in libris horum hominum vitam, et gesta continentibus, hactenus sine recognitione, atque approbatione huiusmodi impressa sunt, nullo modo approbata censeri vult, mandatque Sua Sanctitas.[7]

This decree was incorporated almost verbatim into Urban's Con-

[7] S. C. S. Off., decr. 13 mart. 1625, § 2—*Codicis Iuris Canonici Fontes,* cura Emi Petri Card. Gasparri editi, (9 vols., Romae [postea Civitate Vaticana]: Typis Polyglottis Vaticanis, 1923–1939; Vols. VII–IX, ed. cura et studio Emi Iustiniani Card. Serédi), n. 719 (hereafter cited as *Fontes*).

stitution "*Coelestis Hierusalem.*"[8] It deals with the deeds, miracles, revelations and intercessory powers of the Servants of God, but there is no evidence that these matters were linked in any way with the processes of beatification and canonization. In fact, the opposite seems more probable, for the reservation was entrusted, not to the Sacred Congregation of Rites (the Congregation enjoying competence over these processes), but to the Holy Office.

2. The Decree of 1638

History bears ample witness that the Holy Office exercised this supervision; for example, a decree of 1638 may be taken:

> Die 3. Iulii 1638. facta relatione EE. et RR. DD. Cardinalibus generalibus Inquisitoribus in Congregatione sancti Officii habita in Conventu S. Mariae super Minervam de multitudine librorum continentium vitas Servorum Dei, qui reperiuntur in Cancellaria sancti Officii, qui iam fuerunt per Religiosos deputatos considerati, dixerunt, remittendos esse ad locorum Ordinarios cum hac epistola, quae inserviat pro responso, de quo in decretis; et semper in posterum formula haec in huiusmodi casibus ad unguem observetur . . . et facta relatione, Sanctissimus approbavit.[9]

This document informs us that a multitude of books was sent and submitted for the approval of the Holy Office. Sooner or later the question was bound to arise: what value could these works, approved by the Holy Office, have in a process of beatification and canonization? Pope Urban settled the question:

> . . . declarando etiam expresse, quod tales libri, seu historiae, licet ab Ordinariis revisae, et post Sedis Apos-

[8] 5 iul. 1634, § 1—*Fontes,* n. 213. The few alterations were not doctrinal but stylistic, necessitated by the change from the form of a decree to that of a Constitution.

[9] S. C. S. Off., 3 iul. 1638. This document, as well as certain documents to be quoted subsequently, is contained neither in the *Fontes* nor in any of the collections of the respective Congregations. Hence it will be necessary to rely on Benedictus XIV, *Opera Omnia* (17 vols., Prati, 1839–1846), Vols. I-VII (*De Servorum Dei Beatificatione, et Beatorum Canonizatione*), lib. II, cap. XI, n. 7 (hereafter cited as Benedictus XIV).

> tolicae responsum approbatae, non faciunt maiorem gradum probationis in ordine ad Canonizationem, seu Beatificationem, quam quae alias absque tali approbatione de iure fecissent, non obstante quocumque longissimi temporis cursu.[10]

3. The Decree of 1674

The Sacred Congregation of Rites, it appears, took no part in the Roman approval of these books until 1674:

> Consulta sacrorum rituum Congregatione per Reverendiss. P. Magistrum sacri Palatii super modo concedendi licentiam imprimendi libros continentes vitas, gesta, et miracula Servorum Dei non adhuc a Sede Apostolica Sanctorum fasti adscriptorum, eadem sacra Congregatio censuit, in posterum, antequam typis mandentur, revidendos esse per R. P. D. fide Promotorem, et per eumden in sacrorum rituum Congregatione referendos: Hac die 17 novembris 1674.[11]

In this decree nothing is mentioned about a transfer of the approval of these books from the Holy Office to the Sacred Congregation of Rites. The term *revidendos* suggests that the Holy Office still maintained its former position, but was supplemented in some way by the Congregation of Rites. The "*in sacrorum rituum Congregatione referendos*" suggests that the only task of the Congregation of Rites was to keep a record of all these books for the purpose of having a list on hand should a process be initiated.

4. The Decree of 1757

At the time of Benedict XIV (1740–1758), however, the Congregation of Rites seems to have been exercising full control over these books:

> Sacra Rituum Congregatio aliquando eorumdem revisionem defert ad Congregationem SSmae Inquisitionis, quae, accepta relatione ab aliquo ex suis Relatoribus aut Qualificatoribus, si quando illa typis imprimendi facul-

[10] Decr. gen., 12 mart. 1642—Benedictus XIV, lib. II, Appendix prima.

[11] S. R. C., decr. 17 nov. 1674—Benedictus XIV, lib. II, cap. XI, n. 7.

tatem tribuit, iniungit locorum Ordinariis observantiam erga saepe memorata Decreta Urbani VIII.[12]

5. The Decree of 1821

A final decree, in 1821, revealed the fact that the decree of 1625, the Constitution of 1634 and the decree of 1674 were no longer being observed, and that the Congregation of Rites restated the former law to insist on its observance:

> Salutaria haec instituta paullatim languescere ac ex usu plane iam decessisse compertum est; ideoque S. R. C. Secretarius, de opportuno remedio adhibendo egit in generali Conventu habito die 28 iulii 1821. Re itaque diligenter perpensa, Emi PP. decernendum censuere: " Detur novum Decretum, facto verbo cum SSmo; et transmittatur ex Officio P. M. S. Palatii Apostolici."
>
> Facta autem de praemissis omnibus SSmo D. N. Pio VII Pont. Max. relatione per infrascriptum Secretarium, Sanctitas Sua Sacrae Congregationis Decretum approbavit et confirmavit; ac ut ab omnibus servetur, typis evulgari atque in actis eiusdem Congregationis referri mandavit.[13]

However, history gives evidence that this decree was not observed, even after 1821. The local ordinaries continued to approve these works and failed to forward them to Rome for the approval of the Sacred Congregation of Rites.[14] Finally, when Pope Leo XIII (1878–1903) reorganized the entire matter on the censorship of books in his Constitution *"Officiorum ac munerum,"* the decree of 1625, the Constitution of 1634, and the decrees of 1674, 1757 and 1821 concerning the publication of the

[12] This decree of 1757 is quoted in S.R.C., decr. gen., 31 iul. 1821—*Decreta Authentica Congregationis Sacrorum Rituum ex actis eiusdem collecta eiusque auctoritate promulgata sub auspiciis SS. Domini nostri Leonis Papae XIII* (5 vols. et 2 Appendices, Romae, 1898–1927), n. 2617 (hereafter cited as *Decr. Auth.*).

[13] 31 iul. 1821—*Fontes,* n. 5843; *Decr. Auth.,* n. 2617.

[14] Boudinhon, *La Nouvelle Législation de l'Index* (2. ed., Paris, 1925), p. 232 (hereafter cited as *Nouv. Législ.*); Pennacchi, "In Constitutionem Apostolicam '*Officiorum ac munerum*' brevis commentatio"—*Acta Sanctae Sedis* (41 vols., Romae, 1865–1908), XXX (1897–1898), 481 (hereafter cited as *ASS*).

lives, deeds, miracles, etc., of the Servants of God were omitted entirely. Hence, these matters were no longer reserved to the Congregation of Rites.[15] Similarly, the Code made no new law in this matter.

(*b*) *Printing of the Processual Acts*

1. Legislation of Urban VIII (1623–1644)

Parallel to the decrees concerning the deeds, miracles, etc., of the Servants of God, there is another set of decrees concerning the printing of the acts of the processes of beatification and canonization. The first decree, in the order of time, is that of Urban VIII, in 1631. At that time it was mandatory that the acts of the entire process of beatification and canonization be drawn up by hand.[16] It was necessary to make copies of these acts for the use of the members of the Congregation. This task was extremely slow and laborious. Still Pope Urban forbade that these acts be printed:

> Relationes Auditorum Rotae, informationes in facto et in iure, et aliae quaecumque scripturae tractantes de causis Beatificationum et Canonizationum imprimi omnino prohibentur ante earumdem causarum terminationem.[17]

The text does not indicate whether a simple request had been made or whether some official had begun to print these acts on his own authority. The reference to specific portions of the acts, as well as the use of the term *omnino* could possibly be taken as a rebuke; although it could just as well mean that special emphasis is given to the portions named. Whatever the occasion, the decree was decisive.

---

[15] § 35: "Approbatio librorum, quorum censura praesentium Decretorum vi apostolicae Sedi vel Romanis Congregationibus non reservatur, pertinet ad Ordinarium loci in quo publici iuris fiunt."—*Fontes,* n. 632. This Constitution was issued under date of January 25, 1897.

[16] This practice obtains even today for certain portions of the acts, e.g.: "Exemplar processus, seu ut aiunt, *transumptum,* sicut acta archetypa, manu transcribantur."—Canon 2054.

[17] Decr., 31 ian. 1631—Benedictus XIV, lib. I, cap. XIX, n. 18.

2. Legislation of Alexander VII (1665–1667)

Thirty years later Pope Alexander VII (1655–1667) was more liberal. He granted the permission under the following conditions:

> Quamvis fel. record. Urbanus VIII decreto edito die 31 Ianuarii 1631 mox relato, et impresso inter novissima decreta die 12 Martii 1642, pag. 61, in causis Beatificationum et Canonizationum expresse prohibuerit relationes Auditorum Rotae, informationes in facto et in iure, et alias quascumque scripturas tractantes de causis Beatificationum imprimi, ante earundem causarum terminationem; cum tamen experientia fuerit deinde compertum, in illis exemplendis per amanuenses, ob eorum imperitiam vel incuriam, ut plurimum, multa errata irrepere, quae verum illarum sensum immutant, et Postulatores cogi graves impensas subire, quae maxima ex parte minuerentur, si eisdem liceret illas typis mandare; ideo, SS. D. N. Alexander divina providentia Papa VII utrique malo provida solicitudine consulere volens, de consilio, motu proprio, et ex certa scientia, suo speciali decreto indulsit et mandavit, ut in posterum informationes tam in facto quam in iure, summaria, memoralia, oppositiones R. P. D. fidei Promotoris, responsiones, et replicationes, ac omnes et quaecumque aliae scripturae quomodolibet pertinentes ad causas Beatificationum et Canonizationum imprimi et typis mandari possint et valeant, . . . insuper sexaginta tantummodo exemplaria imprimantur, nisi plura desiderentur a Secretario dictae Congregationis sacrorum rituum . . . eadem Sanctitas sua licentiam et facultatem huiusmodi impressionis concessit impressori seu typographo Camerali pro tempore. Quodsi impressor seu typographus Cameralis pro tempore onus imprimendi informationes ac scripturas praedictas pertinentes ad causas Beatificationum, et Canonizationum subire noluit pro pretio . . . tunc Sanctitas sua simul motu proprio, et certa scientia etc. facultatem et licentiam huiusmodi imprimendi dictas informationes, ceterasque omnes et singulas scripturas ad causas Beatificationum, et Canonizationum quomodolibet pertinentes, concessit omnibus et singulis impressoribus seu typographis Urbis pro eodem taxato, ut supra, minorique etiam, si reperiatur, aliisque conditionibus. . . .[18]

[18] 19 iul. 1661—Benedictus XIV, lib. I, cap. XIX, nn. 19–22.

This decree speaks only of a private printing, limited to 60 copies. At the conclusion of the process all copies were to be returned to the Secretary. Anyone retaining a copy (even the printer) was to be punished and fined.

Four days later Pope Alexander issued a further decree, limiting the choice of the printer to the city of Rome:

> Expresse inhibentur omnibus et singulis impressoribus seu typographis ubivis locorum informationes, summaria atque omnes et quascumque alias scripturas pertinentes ad causas beatificationum et canonizatiônum extra Urbem imprimere sub quovis praetextu, causa et quaesito colore et cum quavis auctoritate, licentia et approbatione. Et si quae ausu temerario contra praesentis Decreti tenorem impressa fuerint, omini prorsus fide carere voluit et declaravit sub eiusdem poenis, quae ab Urbano VIII statutae sunt Brev. 5 iul. 1634 contra imprimentes gesta, revelationes et miracula defunctorum cum fama seu opinione sanctitatis sine recognitione et adprobatione Ordinariorum iuxta formam ibi expressam.[19]

It is noteworthy that Alexander applies the same penalties which had been applied by Urban VIII for the unauthorized publication of the lives, etc., of the Servants of God. This is a clear indication that the two were considered as independent pieces of legislation, though parallel.

3. Legislation of Leo XIII (1878–1903)

After the seizure of the Papal States it became increasingly difficult to safeguard the privacy of these processual acts, and hence Pope Leo XIII restated the decrees of Alexander VII to provide for the emergency. He added that only such printers could be chosen who were authorized by the Master of the Sacred Palace:

---

[19] 23 iul. 1661—Benedictus XIV, lib. I, cap. XIX, n. 22. Some writers consider the "scripturas pertinentes ad causas beatificationum et canonizationum" of this decree as the earliest form of canon 1387, e.g., Boudinhon, *Nouv. Législ.*, p. 231; Schneider, *Die neuen Büchergesetze der Kirche* (Mainz, 1900), p. 119 (hereafter cited as *Büchergesetze*); Pennacchi, *ASS*, XXX (1897–1898), 414. Perhaps they were unaware of the similar phrase in the previous decree.

> Sacra Rituum Congregatio Causarum Beatificationis Servorum Dei et Canonizationis Beatorum, quae eius examini proponuntur summam gravitatem perpendens, sui muneris esse duxit illa praecavere pericula, quae ex inconsulta evulgatione eorumdem Servorum Dei rerum gestarum, ac iudicialium desuper disquisitionum, luctuosissimis hisce temporibus, facile oriri possint. Perpensis itaque accurate Decretis sa. me. Alexandri Papae VII diei 19 et 23 Julii anni 1661, statuendum censuit, ut, firma lege nullibi extra Urbem imprimendi quaelibet eiusmodi scripta, in Urbe ipsa, durantibus praedictis rerum publicarum conditionibus, vel donec aliter a Sede Apostolica provisum fuerit, eadem nonnisi a Typographis imprimi valeant, qui ab officio et auctoritate Patris s. Palatii Apostolici Magistri rite dependent, ab eoque approbati habentur. Si secus quaelibet e praefatis scripturis praelo excusa fuerit, tamquam irrita prorsus ac nulla a s. Congregationis Officialibus haberi debeat. Et ita declaravit ac statuit die 30 Ianuarii 1878.
>
> Facta autem de praemissis Sanctissimo Domino Nostro Leoni Papae XIII per me infrascriptum Secretarium fideli relatione, idem Sanctissimus Dominus Noster Decretum S. R. C. praefatum approbavit, et ita servari mandavit. Contrariis non obstantibus quibuscumque. Die 7 Martii anni eiusdem.[20]

Finally, when Leo XIII reorganized the law on the censorship of books, he adopted the gist of the previous decrees as follows:

> Quae ad causas Beatificationum et Canonizationum Servorum Dei utcumque pertinent, absque beneplacito Congregationis Sacris Ritibus tuendis praepositae publicari nequeunt.[21]

The substitution of "*Quae ad causas . . . utcumque pertinent*" for the previous designation of the processual acts by name gave rise to an opinion that the new decree was a fusion of both series; i.e., not only the series in the years 1631, 1661, and 1878 concerning the processual acts, but also the series in the years 1625, 1634, 1638, 1642, 1674, 1757 and 1821 concerning the lives, miracles, etc., of the Servants of God. Pennacchi (+1898) was most vigorous in his insistence on this extension of the law:

---

[20] *ASS,* XI (1878), 366-367.

[21] Const. "*Officiorum ac munerum,*" 25 ian. 1897, § 32—*Fontes,* n. 632.

> "Sciendum videlicet est . . . omnia subdi potestati Promotoris fidei, ita ut praeter huius facultatem, nihil, prorus nihil, de Servo Dei publicari queat, non vita, non biographia, non aliud aliquid, quodcumque illud sit." [22]

Others, however, maintained that there was no real change in the law.[23]

4. Monitum of 1909

Finally, a response of the Congregation of Rites settled the doubt in favor of the traditional view:

> Acta quae respiciunt vitam, virtutes, et prodigia Servorum Dei vel Beatorum, quorum causis manus apposuit S. Rituum Congregatio, typis edi ac publici iuris fieri nequeunt, inconsulta eadem S. Congregatione, et absque licentia *nihil obstat R. P. D.* Promotoris sanctae fidei, vel Adsessoris ipsius sacri Consilii.[24]

5. Canon 1387

The Code adopted the law of Pope Leo with a few slight changes, and hence, for the most part, canon 1387 must be understood in the sense of pre-Code law, that is, as explained by the monitum of 1909. The text of canon 1387 reads:

> Quae ad causas beatificationum et canonizationum Servorum Dei quoquo modo pertinent, sine licentia Sacrorum Rituum Congregationis edi nequeunt.

B. COMMENTARY

Canon 1387 enacts that whatever pertains in any manner to the

[22] *ASS*, XXX (1897-1898), 414. Pennacchi's opinion carried much weight, for he was a consultor of the Congregation, and claimed to have the support of the Promotor of the Faith himself—"In re ipsum sollertissimum Promotorem Fidei interrogavimus."—*loc. cit.*

[23] E.g., Piat, "Commentaire de la Constitution '*Officiorum ac Munerum*' de Sa Sainteté le Pape Léon XIII sur la prohibition et la censure des livres et des décrets généraux qui l'accompagnent"—*Nouvelle Revue Théologique* (Paris, 1869—), XXXII (1900), 10 (hereafter cited as *NRT*); Boudinhon, *Nouv. Législ.*, p. 232; Schneider, *Büchergesetze*, pp. 118-119.

[24] S. R. C., monitum, 12 febr. 1909—*Acta Apostolicae Sedis* (Romae, 1909—), I (1909), 238 (hereafter cited as *AAS*).

causes of beatification and canonization of the Servants of God may not be published without the permission of the Sacred Congregation of Rites. In commenting on this canon, one may advert to the following considerations: (1) the term *causa;* (2) the phrase *quoquo modo pertinent;* (3) the competent authority; (4) censorship; (5) summary.

(1) THE TERM "CAUSA"

A glance at *causa* in the Index of the Code reveals that the term is used in each of the five books of the Code. The Index groups the references into distinct categories under various headings, indicating thereby that *causa* is employed in several different meanings. The *causa* of canon 1387 is found among a host of references to the *causa* of the fourth book of the Code. The meaning of *causa,* then, will be the meaning of *causa* as employed in the fourth book.

Upon investigation it is found that the term *causa* is not defined in the fourth book, nor elsewhere in the Code. Its use in the fourth book is twofold, the one restricted, the other broad. Both are technical uses, and both will be investigated in turn.

(*a*) *The Restricted Meaning of "Causa"*

In its restricted sense, the term *causa* has a long history. As early as the classical period of Roman Law this *causa* appears in court proceedings. From the very beginning it was understood as a controversy brought before a judge to be settled by him.[25] As the centuries passed, this legal term and its definition remained invariable. Both Reiffenstuel (1642–1703)[26] and Schmalzgreuber (1663–1735)[27] bore witness to the stability of the term in this technical sense, and gave almost identical definitions. At the

[25] Gaius, for example (IV, 15), says: ". . . deinde cum ad iudicium venerant, antequam apud eum *causam* perorarent, solebant breviter ei et quasi per indicem rem exponere."—Cogliolo, *Manuale delle Fonti del Diritto Romano* (2. ed., Torino, 1911), p. 318. The italics are in the original.

[26] *Ius Canonicum Universum* (5 vols. in 7, Parisiis, 1864–1870), lib. I, tit. 1, n. 15.

[27] *Ius Ecclesiasticum Universum* (5 vols. in 12, Romae, 1843–1845), lib. I, tit. 1, n. 3.

present time the term appears so well accepted that commentators use it without feeling obliged to define it, e.g., Augustine (1872–1943),[28] Muniz,[29] Roberti[30] and Noval (1861–1938).[31] Lega (1860–1935) defined *causa* as a "ius controversum in iudicium deductum,"[32] while Wernz (1842–1914)-Vidal (1867–1938) gave the following definition: "ipsa controversia quae in iudicium deducitur."[33]

In spite of the long-standing acceptance of the term *causa*, there is reason to believe that the Codifiers modified its meaning in their reorganization of the law.[34] The change was indirect rather than direct consisting in the substitution of "*De Processibus*" for "*De Iudiciis*," the originally drafted heading of the fourth book of the Code. The substituted term now includes three distinct types of legal processes, while the supplanted term was narrowed in its meaning so that it applies exclusively to the first of these processes. Now, while it is possible to adhere to the strict definition of *causa* when one deals with trials, one can hardly adhere to the same strict definition for the term *causa* in its relation to the processes of beatification and canonization, in which there is no controversy in the strict sense and no trial in the proper acceptation of the word. Coronata saw this difficulty. He abandoned the traditional definition of the term *causa* to substitute the following: "a question to be settled by a legal process.[35] This definition is readily

[28] *A Commentary on the New Code of Canon Law* (8 vols., St. Louis, 1918–1922), VII (*Ecclesiastical Trials,* 1921), 387–389 (hereafter cited as *Commentary*).

[29] *Procedimientos Eclesiásticos* (2. ed., 3 vols., Sevilla, 1925), III.

[30] *De Processibus* (2 vols. in 1, Romae, 1926), I, 25–26; 55–56.

[31] *Commentarium Codicis Iuris Canonici,* lib. IV, *De Processibus* (2 vols., Augustae Taurinorum: Marietti, 1920–1932), II, n. 3.

[32] *Praelectiones in Textum Iuris Canonici de Iudiciis Ecclesiasticis in Scholis Pont. Sem. Rom. Habitae* (4 vols. Romae, 1896–1901), I (*De Iudiciis Ecclesiasticis Civilibus*), n. 169.

[33] *Ius Canonicum ad normam Codicis exactum* (7 vols. in 8, Vol. VI, 1927, Romae: Apud Aedes Universitatis Gregorianae, 1923–1938), VI (*De Processibus*), n. 13.

[34] Roberti (*De Processibus,* I, 22–26) recounts the steps of the reorganization and the various motives which led to the change.

[35] "Quaestiones agendae processu iudiciali."—*Institutiones Iuris Canonici* (5 vols., Taurini: Marietti, 1928–1936), III (*De Processibus*), n. 1086 (hereafter cited as *Institutiones*).

applicable to both types of processes, those which are strictly judicial and those which are less strictly judicial. It likewise has the merit of being reasonably authoritative and traditional, for it can be found in Schmalzgrueber [36] and Reiffenstuel.[37] Noval observed that, although the processes of beatification and canonization are not judicial by reason of their matter, they are judicial by reason of their form, and hence merit the designation of "judicial processes." [38] It is also to be noted that a question is pragmatic, i.e., not only an inquiry which seeks an answer, but rather a problem which demands a settlement. With this in mind, the writer accepts Coronata's definition of *causa* in the strict sense as a question to be settled by a legal process.

(*b*) *The Extended Meaning of "Causa"*

The extended meaning of *causa* is of more recent origin. Pre-Code commentators and authors used the term occasionally as a synonym for the term *process,* i.e., a judicial process.[39] A process is defined as a series of juridic acts (*acti legitimi*) established by a competent authority to be observed in the treating and defining of questions.[40] That the Code uses *causa* in this extended meaning is evident. It is found in the inscription above canon 1999, where it is used on a parallel with the term *iudicium* in the inscription above canon 1552. Both are processes. Commen-

---

[36] "Quaestio est ipsa res, vel ius controversum, quod deduci potest in iudicium; quod si actu in iudicium deducatur, causa vocabitur; ut adeo causa et quaestio in hoc solum differant, quod causa proprie non dicatur, nisi in iudicio, quaestio autem extra illud."—lib. I, tit. 1, n. 3.

[37] "Causa tandem proprie dicitur ipsa res controversa, quae in iudicium deducitur. . . . Differt etiam causa a quaestione, quod haec tam intra, quam extra iudicium dicatur; causa vero proprie solum in iudicio."—lib. I, tit. 1, n. 15.

[38] *De Processibus,* II, n. 442.

[39] Cf. Coronata, *Institutiones,* III, n. 1086, n. 1.

[40] This definition is a simplification and fusion of the terminology given by Coronata and Wernz-Vidal. Coronata's definition reads: "Processus est series sollemnitatum iuridicarum in quaestionibus tractandis et negotiis iuridicis expediendis ex publicae auctoritatis sanctione servandarum."—*Loc. cit.* Wernz-Vidal's definition reads: "Series seu complexus actuum legitimorum quibus cognitio et definitio alicuius quaestionis seu negotii ad praescripta legis absolvitur."—*Ius Canonicum,* VI, n. 8.

tators may differ in their definition of the terms, but they are unanimous in using *causa* in the extended sense.

Granted that there are two meanings of *causa,* one strict and the other extended, which is the use of the term in canon 1387? Upon this answer will depend the greater or lesser extension of the entire canon. The answer is quite simple. The *causa* of canon 1387 is to be understood in the extended sense. First, in placing *causa* in canon 1387, the Codifiers would normally be expected to make a reference to a whole rather than to a part, unless the contrary were evident. There is no evidence which lets one believe that the term is to be restricted. Secondly, the very phraseology of the canon, "*Quae ad causas beatificationum et canonizationum Servorum Dei pertinent,*" is an obvious parallel to the inscription above canon 1999, "*De Causis Beatificationis Servorum Dei et Canonizationis Beatorum.*" The *causa* in the inscription must be taken in its extended meaning. Thirdly, the term *causa* is accepted as having a wide meaning in canon 1387 by the commentators. It will be sufficient to make a single reference to a specialist in Code terminology, Koestler, who has published a dictionary of the Code.[41] Fourthly, English commentators use the terms *cause* and *process* indiscriminately. Augustine, in fact, uses the terms *trial, cause* and *process* with little or no difference of meaning.[42] Woywod (1880–1941) is an interesting example, for in publishing an article on the censorship of books he translated the word *causa* of canon 1387 with the word *process,*[43] whereas in publishing his commentary on the Code he translated the same word with *cause.*[44] For these reasons it appears safe to accept the terms *cause* and *process* as synonymous for the purpose of canon 1387. As a definition the following is accepted: "a series of juridic acts established by a

[41] *Wörterbuch zum Codex Iuris Canonici* (München: F. Pustet, 1927–1929), p. 63.

[42] Cf., e.g., the first several pages of his treatise on the Beatification and Canonization of Saints.—*Commentary,* VII, 385–390.

[43] "Law of the Code—Ecclesiastical Censorship"—*Homiletic and Pastoral Review* (New York, 1900—) XXVIII (1928), 866 (hereafter cited as *HPR*).

[44] *A Practical Commentary on the Code of Canon Law* (3. ed., 2 vols., New York: J. Wagner, 1929), II, n. 1402 (hereafter cited as *Commentary*).

competent authority to be observed in the treating and defining of questions."

(2) THE PHRASE "QUOQUO MODO PERTINENT"

Canon 1387 requires the permission of the Sacred Congregation of Rites for the publication of anything that pertains in any manner—*quoquo modo pertinent*—to the causes of beatification and canonization of the Servants of God. Apparently the phrase "pertains in any manner" is meant to include as much as possible, for there is nothing in the canon to restrict the broad tenor of the law. However, the matter reserved to the Sacred Congregation of Rites is limited in two ways: (a) by the terminology of the canon; and (b) by the competency of the Congregation of Rites.

(*a*) *Matters reserved to the Congregation of Rites are limited by the terminology of the canon.* The *cause,* to which the matters must pertain, is to be accepted in its technical sense, as explained above. As such, it effects a fundamental line of demarcation between those things that pertain to a cause and those things which do not pertain to a cause. It is insufficient to word the canon in any of the two following ways: "pertains to the beatification and canonization," or "pertains to the Servant of God." In the first instance, it is insufficient to say "pertains to the beatification and canonization," for matters may pertain to the beatification and canonization without pertaining to the *cause.* For example, an account of the festivities or solemnities observed in St. Peter's on the day of beatification or canonization could be printed without the permission of the Sacred Congregation of Rites.[45]

In the second instance, it is insufficient to say "pertains to the Servant of God," for there are many things which pertain to a Servant of God which do not pertain to the *cause* of beatification and canonization. For example, the publication of a work contain-

[45] Augustine, therefore, is inaccurate in writing: "Matters pertaining to the canonization and beatification of Servants of God may not be published . . ."—*A Commentary on the New Code of Canon Law* (8 vols., St. Louis, 1918–1922), VI (*Administrative Law,* 1921), 445 (hereafter cited as *Admin. Law*).

ing the admittedly orthodox scientific views of a Servant of God would not be subject to the norm enacted in canon 1387. Similarly, the publication of biographies, books, pamphlets, brochures, articles, leaflets, or any other writings concerning the life, deeds, miracles, revelations, virtues, martyrdom, etc., of the saintly person is allowed. These matters pertain to the Servants of God, and not to the *cause* of beatification and canonization as such.[46]

Authors may not only publish these works, but they may also maintain that the life and virtues of the person were heroic, that the miracles were genuine; they may even call the person a saint, provided that in so doing they advance their opinions as based on criteria of human judgment. Such authors act merely in their private capacity. They may not give the impression that they are acting in the name of the Church, or that their private opinion is the official verdict of the Church, until the Church has declared the sanctity of the Servant of God. The authors may be eminent ecclesiastics, and their opinion may carry added weight by reason of their balanced judgment; their opinions, however, remain private opinions. As such, they do not partake of the infallible character of the official judgment of the Church.[47]

An author may draw his material from the usual sources, either public or private, civil or ecclesiastical. There is only one exception. He may not publish the official *acta* of the cause of beatification or canonization of the person in question.[48] Some com-

[46] From 1625 until 1897 the publication of these matters was reserved to Rome. However, this law was certainly abrogated in 1897, as the history of the canon has clearly shown.

[47] All this is evident from the decree (5 iun. 1631), of Urban VIII: "Sanctissimus Dominus Noster mandavit, non debere admitti elogia *Sancti*, vel *Beati* absolute, et quae cadunt super personam; bene tamen posse Magistrum sacri palatii apostolici admittere ea, quae cadunt supra mores et opinionem, cum protestatione in principio, quod his nulla adsit auctoritas ab Ecclesia Romana, sed fides tantum sit penes Auctorem."—Benedict XIV, lib. II, cap. XII, n. 2. Although this decree was a private response to the Capuchin Order, it was extended and applied universally, not only to the name "Saint" or "Blessed," but also to the miracles, revelations, etc. Since 1897 the reservation in this law is no longer in effect, in consequence of the fact that it was left unmentioned in the Constitution "*Officiorum et munerum.*"

[48] This is the meaning of *Quae ad causas quoquo modo pertinent,* as

mentators merely state that the *acta* may not be published without permission from the Sacred Congregation of Rites.[49] Others distinguished between the *acta causae,* which are original for every Servant of God,[50] and the *acta processus,*[51] which are identical (save for a change of names, etc.) in all causes.[52] De Meester, Ayrinhac, Blat, Noldin-Schmitt, Laurentius, Boudinhon, Piat, Gennari, Jombart, Berutti and Vermeersch hold, either explicitly or implicitly (by the examples they cite), that canon 1387 applies only to the *acta causae.*[53] Schneider (1840–1906) alone held that both were included.[54] The writer holds that canon 1387 applies only to the *acta causae,* and not to the *acta processus.* This

---

appears from the monitum of the Congregation of Rites, 12 febr. 1909—*AAS,* I (1909), 238.

[49] Beste, *Introductio in Codicem* (2 ed., Collegeville: St. John's Abbey Press, 1944), p. 683 (hereafter cited as *Introductio*) ; Pejška, *Ius Canonicum Religiosorum* (3. ed., Friburgi in B.: B. Herder, 1927), p. 171 (hereafter cited as *Ius Canonicum*) ; Ferreres, *Institutiones Canonicae iuxta Novissimum Codicem* (2. ed., 2 vols., Barcinone, 1920), II, n. 388, 1o (hereafter cited as *Institutiones*) ; Aertnys-Damen, *Theologia Moralis secundum doctrinan S. Alfonsi de Ligorio Doctoris Ecclesiae* (14. ed., 2 vols., Taurinorum Augustae: Marietti, 1944), I, n. 1078 (hereafter cited as *Theol. Moral.*) ; Claeys Bouuaert-Simenon, *Manuale Juris Canonici* (3 vols., Vols. I, III, 4. ed., 1934, Vol. II, 2. ed., 1935 Gandae et Leodii: Apud Seminaria) ; III, n. 185 (hereafter cited as *Manuale*) ; Vermeersch-Creusen, *Epitome Iuris Canonici cum commentariis ad scholas et ad usum privatum* (4. ed., 3 vols., Mechliniae-Romae: H. Dessain, 1929–1931), II, n. 725 (hereafter cited as *Epitome*) ; Desjardins, " La Nouvelle Constitution apostolique sur l'Index "—*Études religieuses des PP. Jesuites* (Paris, 1856—), LXXI (1897), 363 (hereafter cited as *Études*).

[50] I.e., those acts which pertain to the merit of the cause, e.g., the depositions of the witnesses and experts concerning the life, virtues, miracles, etc., of the Servant of God, the various proofs, the observations of the consultors, the animadversions of the Promotor of the Faith, etc. Cf. Berutti, *Institutiones Iuris Canonici* (6 vols., Taurini-Romae: Marietti, 1936–1943 [Vol. V adhuc sub praelo]), IV, 428 (hereafter cited as *Institutiones*).

[51] This distinction is made in canon 1642, § 1, where it is prescribed that both be in writing.

[52] I.e., those acts which pertain to the observance of a formality, e.g., the taking of an oath, a citation, the publication of certain decrees concerning the state of the cause, etc. Muñiz (*Procedimientos Eclesiásticos,* III, 675–751) gives a long list of formularies used in processes of beatification and canonization.

[53] De Meester, *Juris Canonici et Juris Canonico-Civilis Compendium* (ed.

opinion appears fully justified in view of the wording of the Monitum of 1909. This decree explained that the text of the law of Leo XIII *Quae ad causas Beatificationum et Canonizationum Servorum Dei utcumque pertinent* was to be understood as meaning *Acta quae respiciunt vitam, virtutes, et prodigia Servorum Dei vel Beatorum.* The Sacred Congregation of Rites, in explaining the law, mentioned only those acts which are *acta causae,* omitting entirely a reference to the *acta processus.*[55] Sufficient authority supports this view, and apparently no author opposes it today.

Certainly, those *acta processus* concerning the progress of the cause of beatification or canonization, which are published in the *Acta Apostolicae Sedis,* are given out in such a manner that they can be reprinted without the permission of the Holy See.[56] This

---

nova, 3 vols. in 4, Brugis: Societas Sancti Augustini, 1921–1928), III, pars 1, n. 1344 (hereafter cited as *Compendium*); Ayrinhac, *Administrative Legislation in the New Code of Canon Law* (New York: Longmans, Green & Co., 1930), p. 282 (hereafter cited at *Admin. Legisl.*); Blat, *Commentarium Textus Codicis Iuris Canonici* (5 vols. in 6, Vol. III, pars 2, 1923, Romae: Ex Typographia Pontificia in Instituto Pii IX, 1919–1927), III, pars 2, n. 274 (hereafter cited as *Commentarium*); Noldin-Schmitt, *Summa Theologiae Moralis* (27. ed., 3 vols., Oeniponte-Lipsiae: F. Rauch, 1941–1942), II, n. 700 (hereafter cited as *Summa*); Laurentius, *Institutiones Iuris Ecclesiastici* (3. ed., Friburgi in B., 1914), n. 637, 2o (hereafter cited as *Institutiones*); Boudinhon, *Nouv. Législ.*, p. 232; Piat, *NRT*, XXXII (1900), 10; [Génnari], "Circa la Nuova Disciplina sulla Proibizione e Sulla Censura de' Libri"—*Il Monitore Ecclesiastico* (Romae, 1876—), X, pars 1 (1897), 107 (hereafter cited as *Monit. Eccl.*); Jombart, "Censures des Livres"—*Dictionnaire de Droit Canonique* (Paris: Librairie Letouzey et Ané, 1924—) III, fasc. 13 (1938), col. 162 (hereafter cited as *DDC*); Berutti, *Institutiones*, IV, 428; Vermeersch, *De Prohibitione et Censura Librorum Dissertatio canonico-moralis* (4. ed., Romae, 1906), n. 107 (hereafter cited as *De Prohibitione*).

[54] *Büchergesetze,* p. 120. It must be remembered that Schneider wrote in 1900, at a time when there still was considerable doubt about the exact meaning of the law.

[55] The primary purpose of the Monitum, however, was merely to declare that the life and virtues and miracles as such were not contemplated by the law, but only the official acts pertaining to these matters.

[56] "Cette interdiction [can. 1387] . . . n'etteint pas les informations et renseignements sur l'état d'une cause, ni la reproduction des décrets émanés de la S. C. dans ces sortes de procès"—Boudinhon, *Nouv. Législ.*, p. 232; Blat, *Commentarium,* III, pars 2, n. 275; De Meester, *Compendium,* III, pars 1, n. 1344; Pennacchi, *ASS,* XXX (1897–1898), 413; Piat, *NRT,* XXXII (1900), 10; Génnari, *Monit. Eccl.*, X, pars 1 (1897), 107.

does not appear to be an exception as much as an implicit granting of permission by the very fact that the Congregation of Rites publishes these decrees. The only condition that is necessary, as with the re-publication of decrees of all Roman Congregations whose authenticity is guaranteed by a public document, is the *Imprimatur* of the local ordinary (canon 1389).

An author may even publish the *acta causae* if he obtains permission from the Congregation of Rites. One of the officials of the Congregation uses these acts during the process to write a "*Vita*" of the person to be beatified or canonized.[57]

The failure to observe this basic distinction between the acts of a cause and the matters which pertain merely to the Servants of God results in much needless confusion. There may have been some excuse for Pennacchi's failure to grasp this distinction in 1897, for the doubt of law was clarified only in 1909 by means of the *monitum* of the Congregation of Rites. But there is no adequate excuse for Woywod's view, some twenty years later:

> After the introduction [of the cause] there [at the Sacred Congregation of Rites], such publications [books, pamphlets, and leaflets which deal with the life and character of a saintly person] are reserved to the approval of the said Congregation (Cfr. *Monitum* of 1909). As to miracles which are believed to have been wrought at the intercession of a saintly deceased person, the Holy See does not permit their publication in books, magazines, pamphlets, etc., except by permission of the Sacred Congregation of Rites, as may be gathered from the various decrees of the Holy See on this matter (cfr. *Codex pro Postulatoribus,* by the Postulator General O.F.M., Appendix, pp. 255–288).[58]

[57] "Historia vitae novensilis Beati [Sancti] conscribenda est, eiusque compendium, quae sunt typis vulganda et distribuenda. Tum in *Vita* tum in compendio, de Causae Actis mentio fieri solet, ac potissime de Miraculis quae adprobata fuere. Qui *Vitam* aut compendium describit, omittet protestationes quae in eiusmodi libris scribi debent cum de Servis Dei agitur Coelitum honoribus non auctis; sed scriptum vulgari nequit nisi R. Congregationis Assessor id permiserit"—*Codex pro Postulatoribus Causarum Beatificationis et Canonizationis* editio quarta ad novi Juris Canonici normas exacta cura postulationis generalis Ordinis Fratrum Minorum (Romae: Libreria del Collegio S. Antonio, 1929), pp. 268; 281 (hereafter cited as *Codex pro Postulatoribus*).

[58] Woywod, *HPR,* XXVIII (1928), 866–867.

The *monitum* cited as the source for the first sentence states expressly that the reservation concerns only the processual acts (*acta*) of the life, virtues, and miracles of a Servant of God. It does not concern the life, virtues, and miracles as such. Similarly, the Appendix to the *Codex pro Postulatoribus,* cited as a source for the second sentence, is nothing more than a collection of Roman documents and decrees. Woywod's opinion was taken from the decree of 1625, which had been abrogated by Leo XIII as far as this particular reservation was concerned.

Woywod also maintained in his *Commentary*[59] that canon 1387 is based on the decrees of 1625 and 1821, and the constitutions of 1634 and 1897, inasmuch as these are cited in the Code as footnotes to that canon. The decrees of 1631, 1661, and 1878 are not mentioned in the footnote to canon 1387. At times it is permissible to argue from the footnotes in the Code to the text of the canon, but in the present instance such argumentation is unwarranted in view of the textual development of the canon, the voice of tradition and the contemporary agreement of canonists.

The correct stand in this matter is the one which Woywod himself expressed in the very same article referred to above:

> The Church does not forbid us to make known the life and virtues of Servants of God who departed this life with the reputation of sanctity. In fact, if they remained unknown to the Catholic world, one could hardly expect that the cause of these Servants of God would ever come to a successful end. Miracles are required as part of the proofs of sanctity of the Servants of God, and, unless people asked the intercession of these saintly men and women in their needs, there would, ordinarily speaking, be no miracles. Wherefore, the Postulator General of the Order of Friars Minor recently (April 1, 1927) addressed by circular letter the Provincials of the Order and the Vice-Postulators to excite the devotion and confidence of the people towards the Servants of God in word and *in writing.*[60]

---

[59] II, n. 1402.

[60] Emphasis added. Woywod offered no explanation of how he reconciled this opinion with the opinion quoted above. Taken together these two pas-

(*b*) *Matters reserved to the Sacred Congregation of Rites are limited by the competency of that Congregation.* The Sacred Congregation of Rites has power to reserve permission for the publication of a cause of beatification or canonization only during the time that it has jurisdiction over that cause. There is a definite moment when that jurisdiction begins, and a definite moment when that jurisdiction ends.

A cause of beatification begins at the Sacred Congregation of Rites when the Promoter of the Faith, acting in the name of the Congregation, receives[61] the *transumptum*[62] of the informative process conducted by the local ordinary.[63] The designation of this moment as the beginning of the jurisdiction of the Sacred Congregation of Rites is not arbitrary. It is contained explicitly in the *Monitum* of that Congregation, dated 1909:

> Acta quae respiciunt vitam, virtutes, et prodigia Servorum Dei vel Beatorum, quorum causis beatificationis et canonizationis *manus apposuit S. Rituum Congregatio* typis edi ac publici iuris fieri nequeunt, inconsulta eadem S. Congregatione. . . .[64]

Commentators before and after the Code agree on the same designation.[65] Until the Promoter of the Faith receives the *transump-*

---

sages form his complete commentary to canon 1387, as given in *HPR*, XXVIII (1928), 866–867.

[61] The formality of receiving (canons 2063, § 1, and 2065) is not to be identified with the formality of beginning the cause in Rome (canon 2083), which occurs at a later date.

[62] According to canon 2054, the *transumptum* is the dossier gathered and composed in the tribunal of the local ordinary during the informative process. It is a technical name given to the *acts* of this process.

[63] The Code outlines three distinct processes to be conducted by the local ordinary, namely: (1) the examination of the writings of the Servant of God (canons 2042–2048); (2) the informative process, i.e., the inquiry into the repute of sanctity, the miracles, and, if apropos, the martyrdom of the Servant of God (canons 2049–2056); (3) the investigation of the non-cult of the Servant of God (canons 2057–2064). Acts are composed and gathered for each of these three processes. The *transumptum* refers exclusively to the acts of the second process.

[64] *AAS*, I (1909), 238. Emphasis added.

[65] Some advert to the point explicitly, e.g., Pennacchi, *ASS*, XXX (1897–1898), 414; Piat, *NRT*, XXXII (1900), 10; Blat, *Commentarium*, III, pars

tum, the publication of the processual acts of the local ordinary is not reserved by canon 1387, but is within the full control of the local ordinary. This does not imply that the local ordinary is free to publish these matters according to the ordinary rules of censorship, even though he is conducting the process in his own right (*iure proprio*) in virtue of canons 1999, §3, and 2039, §1. His liberty is circumscribed by other canons in the Code, e.g. canon 2041, §2:

> Post unamquamque sessionem acta causae claudi et iudicis sigillo obsignari debent, non aperienda, nisi in sequenti sessione, postquam iudex sigillum integrum et intactum recognoverit; si sigillum integrum et intactum non inveniatur, iudex rem deferat ad Sacram Congregationem,"

and canon 2056, §§1, 2:

> § 1. Absoluta collatione archetypum clauditur et sigillis munitur in archivo Curiae diligenter asservandum et nunquam aperiendum sine venia Sedis Apostolicae.
>
> § 2. Transumptum vero clauditur et obsignatur sigillo Ordinarii atque hac de re notarius instrumentum in duplici exemplari conficit alterum Romam transmittendum, alterum in archivo Curiae asservandum.

Furthermore, all persons involved in these processes are subjected to the greatest secrecy, so that there is no legitimate way of publishing the acts without the permission of the Sacred Congregation of Rites.[66] This secrecy must be observed until the publication of the process.[67]

2, n. 275; Ferreres, *Institutiones,* II, n. 388, 1º. Other commentators repeat, more or less literally, the wording of the *Monitum,* e.g., Claeys Bouuaert-Simenon, *Manuale,* III, n. 185; Wernz-Vidal, *Ius Canonicum,* IV, pars 2, n. 711. Still others demand that the cause be pending at the Sacred Congregation of Rites before the reservation begins, e.g., Boudinhon, *Nouv. Législ.,* p. 232; Woywod, *HPR,* XXVIII (1928), 867; Coronata, *Institutiones,* III, n. 956; Vermeersch-Creusen, *Epitome,* II, n. 725; Beste, *Introductio,* p. 683; Piscetta-Gennaro, *Elementa Theologiae Moralis ad Codicem Iuris Canonici Exacta* (5. ed., 7 vols. in 6, Torino: Società Editrice, 1938–1943), II, n. 125 (hereafter cited as *Elementa*).

[66] Desjardins, *Études,* LXXI (1897), 363–364.

[67] Canon 2037, § 1.

The competency of the Congregation of Rites endures until the process is officially closed, i.e., until the publication of the document of canonization.[68] The process is not closed when the person is declared Venerable, or Blessed.[69] It is merely held in abeyance until the necessary time has elapsed and the new miracles are forthcoming. At the moment of the publication of the decree of canonization the jurisdiction of the Congregation of Rites ceases, since then the process is officially closed. The reservation of canon 1387 also ceases, and the publication of whatever pertained to the cause is now governed by the ordinary rules of censorship.[70] Schneider alone held that the reservation of the law should continue even after the close of the process:

> Allein wir glauben, dass dieses Verbot auch nach Beendigung des Prozesses gilt, und schliessen aus der *ratio legis,* weil es sich hier um authentische Aktenstücke handelt, welche auf kirchliche Glaubwürdigkeit Anspruch machen. . . . Dergleichen Berichte und Erzählungen, welche als historische Thatsachen erzählt werden und nur eine menschliche Glaubwürdigkeit beanspruchen, bedürfen der Approbation des Bishofs; dagegen die Veröffentlichungen aus den Selig- und Heiligsprechungsprozesen der Diener Gottes, welche eine höhere, kirchliche Glaubwürdigkeit beanspruchen, bedürfen der

---

[68] Blat, *Commentarium,* III, pars 2, n. 275; De Meester, *Compendium,* III, pars 1, n. 1344; Sipos, *Enchiridion Iuris Canonici* (Pécs: Ex Typographia "Haladás R.T.," 1926), p. 713, n. 14 (hereafter cited as *Enchiridion*); Wernz-Vidal, *Ius Canonicum,* IV, pars 2, n. 711; Beste, *Introductio,* p. 683; Cocchi, *Commentarium in Codicem Iuris Canonici ad usum Scholarum* (8 vols. in 5, Vol. VI, 2. ed., 1927, Taurini: Marietti, 1920–1930), VI, 151 (hereafter cited as *Commentarium*); Wernz, *Ius Decretalium* (2. ed., 6 vols. in 10, Prati, 1906–1913), III, pars 1, n. 121 (99); Pejška, *Ius Canonicum,* p. 171.

[69] Blat, *Commentarium,* III, pars 2, n. 275.

[70] Pennacchi, *ASS,* XXX (1897–1898), 482; Piat, *NRT,* XXXII (1900), 10; Coronata, *Institutiones,* II, n. 956, 1°; Claeys Bouuaert-Simenon, *Manuale,* III, n. 185; Vermeersch-Creusen, *Epitome,* II, n. 725; De Meester, *Compendium,* III, pars 1, n. 1344; Aertnys-Damen, *Theol. Moral.,* I, n. 1078; Wernz-Vidal, *Ius Canonicum,* IV, pars 2, n. 711; Sipos, *Enchiridion,* p. 713, n. 14; Cocchi, *Commentarium,* VI, 151; Gagnon, *La Censure des Livres* (Les Theses Canoniques de Laval, n. 3, Québec: Université Laval, 1945), n. 221 (hereafter cited as *La Censure*); Vermeersch, *De Prohibitione,* n. 107.

> Erlaubnis der Ritenkongregation. Die einmal veröffentlichten Aktenstücke dürfen späterhin, natürlich unter Gutheissung der Bischöfe, in den Lebensbeschreibungen der Heiligen weiter veröffentlicht und verwertet werden.[71]

It is quite true that canon 1387 (as well as article 32 of the Constitution "*Officiorum ac munerum*") states nothing about the cessation of the reservation. However, Pennacchi discussed all the reasons at length, and concluded that the reservation ceased at the publication of the decree of canonization inasmuch as the jurisdiction of the Congregation of Rites ceased.[72] Pennacchi himself, in the passage cited, urged a continuation of the reservation, but admitted that there was no reservation in the law. A recent example of the publication of the acts of several processes of canonization is the *Acta Canonizationum Quibus Sanctissimus Dominus Noster Pius Papa XI ab anno sacro* 1933 *ad annum* 1935 *Beatis Sanctorum Caelitum Honores Decrevit, cura Alfonsi Carinci Collecta.*[73] It does not contain the permission of the Congregation, nor even an *Imprimatur*.

(3) THE COMPETENT AUTHORITY

In virtue of canon 253, §3, the Sacred Congregation of Rites enjoys exclusive competence over all matters referring to the beatification and canonization of the Servants of God. Canon 1387 concerns only one point—the publication of the official processes of beatification and canonization. The canon entrusts the supervision of the publication to the Sacred Congregation of Rites without any further designation of the person charged with this duty. A decree of the Congregation, however, allots this work to the Promoter of the Faith and to his assistant, the Assessor of the Congregation, also known as the Sub-Promoter of the Faith.[74]

[71] *Büchergesetze*, p. 120.

[72] *ASS*, XXX (1897-1898), 414-415.

[73] The set comprises 2 volumes, was published by Macioce and Pisani in 1939 at the *Insula Liri.*

[74] S. R. C., monitum, 12 febr. 1909—*AAS*, I (1909), 238. Canon 2010, § 2, mentions the duties of both officials, but fails to include this particular activity explicitly.

It is entirely within the competence of the Promoter of the Faith to allow or to disallow the publication of the processes. His authority in this matter begins with the reception of the *transumptum* from the local ordinary, and endures until the termination of the process, i.e., until the publication of the decree of canonization. Pennacchi objected to the liberty of publishing these processual acts after the completion of the process under the ordinary rules of censorship on the grounds that a premature disclosure could easily be prejudicial to persons still living, especially if the saint had lived in recent times.[75] However, he admitted that such a publishing of the processual acts was permitted. There seems to be no special need for a law forbidding the publication. If there is a real need to prolong the secrecy of the processual acts, this can easily be procured by means of a particular decree in a particular instance.

(4) CENSORSHIP

Canon 1387 speaks only of the permission of the Sacred Congregation of Rites. It states nothing about the censorship of the work. However, it is quite evident that as long as the reservation obtains, the censorship of the Sacred Congregation[76] must precede the permission.

The Sacred Congregation of Rites is fully competent to establish conditions to be observed in the publication of the processual acts. It may impose a literal editing of certain portions, it may be satisfied with a substantial conformity with the processual acts, or it may even forbid the publication of certain or all portions of the acts. Pennacchi explained the reasons for such action:

> Plurima in eiusmodi actis intercedunt quae ex vulgi obtutibus amovenda prudenter esse nemo ignorat; ut ex. gr. quando agitur de personis, quae sive bona fide, sive odio

[75] *ASS,* XXX (1897–1898), 482–484.

[76] It is a general rule that the censorship of a work pertains to that authority from whom the permission for its publication is to be sought. Cf. Wernz-Vidal, *Ius Canonicum,* IV, pars 2, n. 709; Vermeersch-Creusen, *Epitome,* II, n. 724; Seraphinus a Loiano, *Institutiones Theologiae Moralis ad normam Iuris Canonici*—(4 vols., Vol. II, 1935, Taurini: Marietti, 1934–1940), II, n. 501 (hereafter cited as *Institutiones*).

> et inimicitia persecutiones, accusationes, calumnias, in Dei Servos excitarunt, illaeque sint dignitate praesertim ecclesiastica praestantes; de monitionibus quibusdam per Dei Servos liberrime exhibitis cuiuscumque dignitatis hominibus, qui bona de caetero existimatione gauderent, nisi his monitionibus eorum vitia in propatulo posita fuissent; de iis quae aliquando Dei Servi a diabolo passint, atque de tentationibus quibus probati fuere, quae aliquando adeo sunt horribiles, ut pene incredibiles videantur; de visionibus, revelationibus, prophetiis editis sive circa privatas personas, sive circa supremos principes et imperia, in quibus aliquando etiam causae indicantur aut concitatae in illos aut superventurae divinae indignationis. Horum autem vaticiniorum plurima, cum aliquando conditioni subiacent, quae homines latet, ideoque aut effectum non sortiuntur, aut tardius sortiuntur, in ludibrium a plurimis vertuntur, et ipsa Servorum Dei sanctitas, quae minime ex his donis gratuitis dependet derisui habeatur. Atque idipsum de visionibus dicatur, quae et intellectus comprehensioni non semel sunt imperviae, et multiplici subiacent interpretationi. Qua de causa prudentiae legibus non admodum conforme videtur haec et alia indiscriminatim publicare, cum ex iis maiora mala quam bona possent oriri. Expediret hinc, ut etiam post confectam Canonizationem S. Rituum Congregationis Praefecti sibi reservarent cognitionem actorum quae publicari vellent, atque bona quidem et utilia permitterent, incongruis vero et inutilibus publicationem denegarent.[77]

Pope Urban VIII had ordained, on June 5, 1631, that an author was obliged to insert a protestation at the beginning of a biography of a Servant of God to the effect that the term "saint," as applied to the person in question, was to be given only human credence. The Church attributed no higher authority to the term until the actual canonization had taken place.[78] In 1642 Pope Urban prescribed a double protestation, one at the beginning, the other at the end of the biography.[79] These prescriptions were binding until 1897, when Pope Leo failed to include them in his Consti-

[77] *ASS,* XXX (1897-1898), 483-484.

[78] Benedictus XIV, lib. II, cap. XII, n. 3.

[79] Decr. gen., 12 mart. 1642—Benedictus XIV, Appendix Prima. Optional formulae were given for both protestations.

tution "*Officiorum ac munerum.*" [80] The Code also omits mention of this protestation. The phrase, "In obedience to the decree of Urban VIII . . . ," is no longer obligatory, and is superfluous.[81]

A book published without the permission of the Sacred Congregation of Rites would not, for that reason alone, be a prohibited book, even though it contained the processual acts of beatification or canonization. Nor would such a book be prohibited if the author failed to observe the conditions prescribed by the Congregation of Rites. This was the law from 1625 until 1897, but it was abrogated by Pope Leo XIII.[82]

(5) SUMMARY

Canon 1387 states that whatever pertains in any manner to the causes of beatification and canonization of the Servants of God may not be published without the permission of the Sacred Congregation of Rites. The history of this canon shows that the law stems from the decrees of 1631, 1661, 1878 and the Constitution of 1897 concerning the publication of the processual acts of the causes of beatification and canonization, rather than from the decree of 1625, the Constitution of 1634, and the decrees of 1638, 1642, 1674, 1757 and 1821 concerning the publication of the lives, miracles, revelations, etc., of the Servants of God. The latter series was abrogated in 1897, and hence these matters may be published today under the ordinary rules of censorship.

The term *causa* in this canon is to be understood in its extended technical sense, i.e., as a synonym for process. It is probable that the canon reserves permission solely for the publishing of the *acta causae*, i.e., the processual acts pertaining to the merits of the cause, and not of the *acta processus*, i.e., the processual acts pertaining to the observance of a formality. Those *acta processus* concerning the status of a cause which the Congregation of Rites

---

[80] De Meester, *Compendium,* III, pars 1, n. 1368; Vermeersch, *De Prohibitione,* n. 79; Lehmkuhl, *Theologia Moralis* (12. ed., 2 vols., Friburgi, 1914), II, n. 1132.

[81] Coronata, *Institutiones,* II, n. 963; Blat, *Commentarium,* III, pars 2, n. 288.

[82] Pennacchi, *ASS,* XXX (1897–1898), 483–484.

publishes in the *Acta Apostolicae Sedis* may be republished under the ordinary rules of censorship.

Permission to publish the processual acts of a cause of beatification or canonization must be sought from the Congregation of Rites (i.e., from the Promoter of the Faith or the Assessor of the Congregation) only while the process is pending at Rome. It begins at Rome when the Promoter of the Faith receives the *transumptum* of the informative process from the local ordinary, and endures until the publication of the decree of canonization. After this latter date the processual acts may be printed under the ordinary rules of censorship, unless the Congregation of Rites has issued a special decree to the contrary.

Censorship is necessary before publication. It pertains to the authority to whom the permission for the publication is reserved. If no special permission is necessary at the time, the censorship is to be performed by the local ordinary. The Congregation of Rites may establish certain conditions to be observed in the publishing of the processual acts. It may demand a literal conformity to certain parts, it may be satisfied with substantial conformity to other portions, and it may demand the omission of still other passages.

The protestation, formerly prescribed by Urban VIII, is no longer obligatory. A book published contrary to the prescription of canon 1387 is not, for that reason alone, a prohibited book.

CHAPTER II

INDULGENCES

(Canon 1388)

Canon 1388 deals with the publication of indulgences. For the most part, indulgences may be printed under the ordinary rules of censorship (§1). However, three special collections of indulgences may not be published without the permission of the Holy See (§2). Each paragraph of this canon will be treated as follows: A. the historical development of the law; B. the commentary.

CANON 1388 §1

> §1. Indulgentiarum libri omnes, summaria, libelli, folia, etc., in quibus earum concessiones continentur, ne edantur sine licentia Ordinarii loci.

A. DEVELOPMENT OF THE LAW ENACTED IN CANON 1388, §1

From time immemorial local bishops were competent to regulate and impart indulgences in their own territories.[1]

(1) LEGISLATION OF THE COUNCIL OF TRENT (1545–1563)

The Council of Trent decreed enactments against abuses of this power, but still left its use within the hands of the bishops. Hence, the verification, vigilance, and the publication of indulgences were so restricted that no new indulgence could be made public in the diocese of a bishop without his previous knowledge and consent.[2]

---

[1] Paulus, in his *Geschichte des Ablasses im Mittelalter, vom Ursprung bis zur Mitte des 14. Jahrhunderts* (2 vols., Paderborn, 1922–1923), presents a very scholarly and detailed study of the entire ecclesiastical institute of indulgences. The classic modern work is that of Beringer-Steinen, *Die Ablässe, ihr Wesen und Gebrauch* (15. ed., 2 vols., Paderborn, 1916–1921); hereafter cited as *Die Ablässe*.

[2] Conc. Trident., Sess. XXV, Continuatio Sessionis, Decretum de indulgentiis.

Almost a century later the Holy Office placed a limitation on the bishops by requiring them to inform the Inquisitors of the content of any new concession, so that the latter might determine whether the indulgence be genuine or false.[3]

(2) LEGISLATION OF CLEMENT IX (1667–1669)

When Pope Clement IX (1667–1669) established the Congregation for Indulgences in 1669,[4] he did so without apparently enacting special rules for its guidance. It may be presumed that the consultors followed the norms which the commission of Cardinals had used previous to that time. Four years after the inception of the Congregation, a case was presented by the Bishop of Cremona, who claimed that the Inquisitor was overstepping his authority in demanding to censor everything that the bishop wished to publish or print. The Inquisitor, basing his stand on the tenth rule of the Tridentine Index, insisted that such was his official duty, and that he intended to carry it out. The Congregation considered the case carefully and gave the following response:

[3] S. C. S. Off., decr. 6 aug. 1653: "Approbationem indulgentiarum et licentiam illas imprimendi spectare ad Ordinarios; sed eosdem Ordinarios teneri communicare tenorem earumdem Indulgentiarum Inquisitoribus ut concorditer videant an sint verae vel falsae"—*ASS,* XXX (1897–1898), 320.

[4] Const. "*In ipsis Pontificatus primordiis,*" 6 iul. 1669—*Bullarum Diplomatum et Privilegiorum Romanorum Pontificum Taurinensis Editio* (24 vols. et Appendix, Augustae Taurinorum, 1857–1872), XVII, 805–806 (hereafter cited as *BRT*). This Congregation was the culmination of a gradual development of the commission of Cardinals established by Clement VIII (1592–1605) in his Const. "*Quaecumque,*" 7 dec. 1604, § 7—*Fontes,* n. 192, and extended by Paul V (1605–1621) in his Const. "*Quae salubriter,*" 3 nov. 1606—*Fontes,* n. 1906. From the year 1669 the Congregation of Indulgences also supervised the question of relics. Pius X (1903–1914) united this Congregation with the Congregation of Rites, placing both under the same Cardinal Prefect and the same Secretary in his motu proprio, 28 ian. 1904—Beringer, *Die Ablässe,* I, 84. A short time later Pius X suppressed this Congregation entirely and entrusted its functions to the Congregation of the Holy Office in his Const. "*Sapienti consilio,*" 29 iun. 1908—*AAS,* I (1909), 7, which Constitution became effective 1 nov. 1908. Finally, Benedict XV (1914–1922), in his motu proprio, 25 mart. 1917—*AAS,* IX (1917), 167, transferred the care of indulgences to the Sacred Penitentiary where it remains today. See also canon 258, § 2.

> Indulgentiae, quas subditis suis Episcopus concedit, et imprimendas curat, tum litterae pastorales, quibus Indulgentias a Summis Pontificibus concessas populo denuntiat, aliaque denique scripta ad regendum populum suum, vel officialium eius nomine promulganda, quae omnia proprie sunt fori episcopalis, in quo iniunguntur poenitentiae et per Indulgentias remittuntur, praeceptaque et dicta feruntur, libera sunt ab Inquisitoris iurisdictione et auctoritate, quo etiam inscio imprimi possunt: sed de reliquis Episcopus ad Inquisitorem communicare debet, antequam imprimantur.[5]

(3) LEGISLATION OF BENEDICT XIV (1740–1758)

When Pope Benedict XIV (1740–1758) published the Index of Forbidden Books he also published a Constitution to regulate the method of examining and proscribing books for the future, as well as a set of decrees concerning such forbidden books as were not mentioned in the Index. The decree pertaining to indulgences gives ample evidence that canon 1388, § 1, is derived from it:

> Indulgentiarum libri omnes, diaria, summaria, libelli, folia, etc., in quibus earum concessiones continentur, non edantur absque licentia S. Congregationis Indulgentiarum.[6]

From the wording of the decree one would gather that the Sacred Congregation reserved to itself exclusively the power to grant permission for the publication of these indulgences. However, the decree did not explicitly revoke the power of the local ordinaries, nor did it expressly mention the exclusive jurisdiction

---

[5] S. C. Indulg., decr. 24 iul. 1673—*Decreta Authentica Sacrae Congregationis Indulgentiis Sacrisque Reliquiis praepositae ab anno 1668 ad annum 1882 edita, iussu et auctoritate Sanctissimi D. N. Leonis Pp. XIII* (Ratisbonae-Neo Eboraci & Cincinnatii, 1883), n. 8 (hereafter cited as *Decr. Auth. Indulg.*).

[6] Benedictus XIV, const. "*Sollicita ac provida,*" 9 iul. 1753—*Fontes*, n. 426; also *Decreta de libris prohibitis nec in Indice nominatim expressis*, § 3, n. 12, in *Index Librorum Prohibitorum, iuxta exemplar Romanum, iussu Sanctissimi Domini Nostri Leonis XIII Pontificis Maximi editum anno MDCCCLXXXIV editio novissima* (Mechliniae, 1893), p. xxxiv (hereafter cited *Index Leonis XIII*).

of the Sacred Congregation; hence, the bishops continued to use the power they had theretofore enjoyed. And, when a case was brought up for settlement, the Congregation itself gave a favorable reply for the ordinaries. As early as 1760 the Sacred Congregation of the Council took this power of the local bishops for granted in vindicating the claims of a certain bishop against an abbot.[7] The Congregation of Indulgences, too, admonished the bishops to be vigilant in the printing and publication of indulgences, particularly to prevent the spread of apocryphal and false indulgences and concessions.[8]

(4) LEGISLATION OF LEO XIII (1878–1903)

Finally, Pope Leo XIII (1878–1903) reorganized the legislation concerning the censorship of books, and took up the question of indulgences in article 17 of his Constitution "*Officiorum ac munerum*":

> Indulgentiarum libri omnes, summaria, libelli, folia, etc., in quibus earum concessiones continentur, non publicentur absque competentis auctoritatis licentia.[9]

It is readily discernible that no mention was made of the Sacred Congregation of Indulgences. The article spoke merely of the competent authority.[10] For the rest, the new decree was almost identical with the earlier decree.

(5) CANON 1388, § 1

The present Code of Canon Law adopted the decree of Leo XIII, but improved the text by making the designation of the competent authority more explicit. It asserts that this power is completely within the jurisdiction of the local ordinary:

---

[7] S. C. C., *Aquilana,* 10 maii, 7, 21 iun. 1760—*Fontes,* n. 3700.

[8] S. C. Indulg., *Urbis et Orbis,* 14 apr. 1856—*Fontes,* n. 5057; *Decr. Auth. Indulg.,* n. 371.

[9] 25 ian., 1897—*Fontes,* n. 632.

[10] The Sacred Congregation of Indulgences immediately made a public statement to the effect that what before had been reserved to the Congregation remained reserved. Cf. S. C. Indulg., decr. 7 aug. 1897—*ASS,* XXX (1897-1898), 195.

Indulgentiarum libri omnes, summaria, libelli, folia, etc., in quibus earum concessiones continentur, ne edantur sine licentia Ordinarii loci.

B. Commentary

The commentary on the first paragraph of canon 1388 will be divided as follows: (1) the matter to be submitted; (2) the competent authority; (3) censorship; (4) exceptions.

(1) THE MATTER TO BE SUBMITTED

Canon 1388, § 1, mentions several classes of works to be submitted to the local ordinary, namely, all books,[11] collections,[12] booklets,[13] leaflets,[14] etc.[15] The inclusion of *etc.* indicates that the list is not all-inclusive. The law includes the publication of each and every indulgence. The reason is quite obvious—to safeguard the faithful from the publication of false, apocryphal or exaggerated indulgences,[16] and also to prevent the publication of indulgences on private authority.[17]

---

[11] "Libri omnes, i.e. qui nempe illarum [indulgentiarum] tractatum vel denunciationes contineant."—Blat, *Commentarium,* III, pars 2, n. 276; "variarum Indulgentiarum concessiones in volumen compactae atque publicatae."—Pennacchi, *ASS,* XXX (1897–1898), 318.

[12] "Summaria, i.e. similium concessionum circa devotionem aliquam, confraternitatem, etc."—Blat, *loc. cit.;* "sunt compendia, quibus variae Indulgentiae indicantur, earumque concessionum decreta citantur, aut breviter referuntur, quin ad verbum allegantur."—Pennacchi, *loc. cit.* The collections mentioned in § 1 are all those not included under § 2 of this canon.

[13] "Libelli, i.e. ob parvitatem eorum."—Blat, *loc. cit.;* "sunt parvae molis libri, quibus concessae Indulgentiae paucae plerumque absque vel cum adnexis decretis referuntur, et Christifidelibus commendantur."—Pennacchi, *loc. cit.*

[14] "Folia, i.e. quae unam vel alteram orationem indulgentiis ditatam edicunt."—Blat, *loc. cit.;* "constant duobus vel pluribus paginis iuxta editionis magnitudinem quam quis adoptat, in folio, in 4o, in 8o, in 16o, in 24o, quibus aliqua Indulgentia proponitur, et pietati fidelium commendatur."—Pennacchi, *loc. cit.*

[15] "Scriptum quodcumque, etsi unica pagina constet dumtaxat."—Beste, *Introductio,* p. 683; De Meester, *Compendium,* III, pars 1, n. 1345; Boudinhon, *Nouv. Législ.,* p. 169.

[16] Pennacchi, *ASS,* XXX (1897–1898), 327.

[17] Woywod, *Commentary,* II, n. 1403.

(2) THE COMPETENT AUTHORITY

The canon places the supervision of all the above-mentioned indulgences within the competence of the local ordinary, the *Ordinarius loci.* Immediately there is room for discussion, since the Code does not determine explicitly *which place.* Opinion is divided, and commentators are accumulating on both sides. One group maintains that the local ordinary is the ordinary of the place where the indulgence is to be published. The second group favors the liberty of choosing one of the three local ordinaries mentioned in canon 1385, § 2.

The first view regards the local ordinary of the place of publication as the only competent authority to grant permission. Vermeersch (1858-1936)-Creusen base their stand on the word-position within the canon.[18] This reason is accepted without comment by several.[19] Vermeersch-Creusen add that the pre-Code law demanded this view,[20] while all other commentators fail to give a reason for their opinion.[21]

Commentators who favor the liberty of choosing between the three local ordinaries mentioned in canon 1385, § 2, are even more meager in giving their reason for holding their opinion. Most of them mention no reason at all.[22] Only Tummulo-Iorio venture an argument from canon 20.[23]

---

[18] " Si attendas ad verba c. 1388, § 1, respondebis: loci ubi publici iuris fiunt [indulgentiae], cum vocabulum 'edantur' duobus tantum vocabulis separetur a vocabulo: Ordinarius loci "—*Epitome,* II, n. 726, 3o.

[19] E.g., De Meester, *Compendium,* III pars 1, n. 1345; Ubach, *Theologia Moralis Codici Juris Canonici accomodatum* (2. ed., 2 vols., Bonis Auris: Sociedad San Miguel, 1935), I, 558 (hereafter cited as *Theol. Moral.*).

[20] *Epitome,* II, n. 726, 3o.

[21] E.g., Beste, *Introductio,* p. 683; Ayrinhac, *Admin. Legisl.,* p. 282; Wernz-Vidal, *Ius Canonicum,* IV, pars 2, n. 712.

[22] E.g., Blat, *Commentarium,* III, pars 2, n. 276; Sipos, *Enchiridion,* p. 713, n. 15; Prümmer, *Manuale Iuris Canonici in usum Scholarum* (3. ed., Friburgi Brisgoviae, 1922), q. 416 (hereafter cited as *Manuale*); Coronata, *Institutiones,* II, n. 956, 2o; Woywod, *HPR,* XXVIII (1928), 868; Seraphinus a Loiano, *Institutiones,* II, n. 502; Jombart, *DDC,* III, col. 163; Gallik, *The Rights and Duties of Bishops Regarding Diocesan Sisterhoods* (St. Paul: The Wanderer Printing Co., 1939), p. 112; Bouscaren-Ellis, *Canon Law, A Text and Commentary* (Milwaukee, Bruce Publ. Co., 1946), p. 709 (hereafter cited as *Canon Law*).

[23] " Id suadet, inter alia, generalis regula interpretationis de qua in can.

To the writer, the second view favoring greater liberty seems preferable for the following reasons:

(1) Canon 1388, § 1, does not read "*Ordinarius loci ubi publici iuris fiunt*" but merely "*Ordinarius loci.*" Where the Code does not distinguish, and where the Code does not limit liberty, neither should a commentator.[24]

(2) Even though the pre-Code law limited the choice of the local ordinary to the place of publication, the new law does not. If Vermeersch-Creusen, De Meester and Ubach present this as an argument, they must show that the law remained unchanged. The fact is, the law was changed. The "*non publicentur*" of the pre-Code law was altered to read "*ne edantur*" in canon 1388, § 1.[25]

(3) Canon 1385, § 2, is relatively new in the law. Although it refers only to § 1 of the same canon explicitly,[26] it refers to canon 1388, § 1, implicitly. For canon 1388, § 1, is nothing more

20.—Alii tamen aliter opinantur."—*Compendium Theologiae Moralis* (2 vols. & Suppl., Neapoli: M. D'Auria, 1934–1936), *Supplementum* (*De Censuris, Prohibitione Librorum, Irregularitatibus, Indulgentiis*), n. 1002, note 1 (hereafter cited as *De Censuris*).

[24] Woywod, *HPR*, XXVIII (1928), 868.

[25] The real force of the change of terms lies in the fact that from the time of Benedict XIV (1740–1758) until the time of Leo XIII (1878–1903) the term "*edantur*" was used exclusively for the local ordinary of the place of printing. Leo XIII adopted the law of Benedict XIV almost verbatim; one notable change was the deletion of "*edantur*" and the substitution of "*publicentur,*" which all commentators understood as a substitution of the local ordinary of the place of publication for the local ordinary of the place of printing. The Code, however, reverted to the term "*edantur.*" Vermeersch-Creusen, De Meester and Ubach failed to observe this change. Even had they done so, it is inconceivable that they would have interpreted it to mean a reversion to the local ordinary of the place of printing. No commentator today, as far as is known, interprets canon 1388, § 1, as pointing solely to the local ordinary of the place of printing. The only plausible reason, it seems, for changing "*publicentur*" to "*edantur*" is to indicate that the new law no longer restricts the choice to the local ordinary of the place of publication. For a more elaborate discussion of the pre-Code law see Desjardins, *Études*, LXXI (1897), 364.

[26] "Licentiam edendi libros et imagines *de quibus in § 1* dare potest vel loci Ordinarius proprius auctoris, vel Ordinarius loci in quo libri vel imagines publici iuris fiant, vel Ordinarius loci in quo imprimantur." Italics added.

than a restatement of the general rule expressed in canon 1385, § 1.[27]

(4) The argument drawn from the word-position of this canon is, at best, extremely tenuous. The text resists any other word position save placing "*ne edantur*" at the head of the paragraph, which would place greater emphasis on the act of publication. In any event, the nuance is too elusive to support the interpretation desired.

(5) The purpose of the law, i.e., the verification of the indulgence by a public ecclesiastical authority, is sufficiently safeguarded by the censorship of any of the three local ordinaries.

These five reasons establish sufficiently that canon 1388, § 1, does not restrict the choice of the local ordinary to the local ordinary of the place of publication; they show, rather, that the canon allows the choice of any of the three local ordinaries mentioned in canon 1385, § 2.[28]

(3) CENSORSHIP

Canon 1388, § 1, deals with the obtaining of permission from the local ordinary, but fails to mention anything about censorship. It is evident that the local ordinary may not grant the permission (*Imprimatur*) until the censorship has taken place. In this instance the term permission includes both.

The duty of the censor is to examine the intended publication to investigate the indulgences contained therein, and to establish their reliability by verifying them. He must be assured of the perfect conformity of the indulgence mentioned with the indulgence actually granted. The authentic document which serves as a basis for comparison may be the original document of grant, e.g., a

---

[27] Si le paragraphe premier de ce canon [1388], en remettant à l'approbation épiscopale les publications,—évidement religieuses,—d'indulgences, répète la règle du canon 1385, c'est pour amener et mieux faire comprendre l'exception du paragraphe suivant—Gagnon, *La Censure,* n. 224; Jombart, *DDC,* III, col. 163.

[28] Some authors evade the issue, e.g., Sabetti-Barrett, *Compendium Theologiae Moralis* (34. ed., Neo Eboraci-Cincinnati: F. Pustet, 1939), p. 336 (hereafter cited as *Compendium*); Cocchi, on the other hand, mentions both views, but declines to adopt specifically either of them.—*Commentarium,* VI, 152.

rescript; it may be an authentic collection of indulgenced prayers, e.g., the Raccolta; it may be any other current collection of indulgences approved by the Holy See, or, at least, by another bishop; it may be, finally, the publication of the grant in the official organ of the Holy See, the *Acta Apostolicae Sedis.*[29]

The Holy See has given detailed instructions and criteria to aid the censor in forming his judgment. The general rules are found in a decree of the Sacred Congregation of Indulgences, 10 aug. 1899—*ASS,* XXXII (1899–1900), 241–244. The pages immediately following [244–249] are devoted to a commentary on these rules. More specific decrees are dated 26 maii, 1898—*ASS,* XXXI (1898–1899), 127-128; 727-744.

Indulgences published without the requisite permission are not, for that reason alone, prohibited. This problem will be dealt with more fully in the commentary on § 2 of canon 1388.

(4) EXCEPTIONS

Although canon 1388, § 1, forbids the publication of indulgences without the permission of the local ordinary, still, one exception is admitted. The permission of the local ordinary is not required for the publication of indulgences, of indulgenced prayers, or of indulgenced ejaculations on remembrance cards or souvenirs distributed on the occasion of an ordination, a First Mass, a funeral, a consecration, a religious or sacerdotal jubilee, a solemn Communion, a church festival, or any similar occasion.

All commentators admit this exception. Several base this exemption on custom.[30] Others advance the reason that the distribution is limited to a select group rather than being made available to the public at large.[31] As such, it could be called a private print-

[29] S. C. Indulg., *Petrocoren.,* 22 ian. 1858—*Decr. Auth. Indulg.,* n. 383—*Fontes,* n. 5059. Also see Cance, *Le Code de Droit Canonique* (2. ed., 3 vols., Paris: Librairie Lecoffre, 1929), III, 159 (hereafter cited as *Le Code*); Coronata, *Institutiones,* II, n. 956, 2°; Woywod, *HPR,* XXVIII (1928), 868.

[30] E.g., De Meester, *Compendium,* III, pars 1, n. 1345 note 5; Vermeersch, *De Prohibitione,* n. 87; Marc-Gestermann-Raus, *Institutiones Morales Alphonsianae seu Doctoris Ecclesiae S. Alphonsi Mariae de Ligorio Doctrina Moralis ad usum Scholarum accomodata* (18. ed., 2 vols., Lugduni: E. Vitte, 1927), II, 855 (hereafter cited as *Institutiones*).

[31] Beste, *Introductio,* p. 683; Boudinhon, *Nouv. Législ.,* p. 170; Gagnon, *La Censure,* n. 226.

ing. Jombart admits this exception on the basis of the axiom "*parvum pro nihilo reputatur.*" [32] By far the majority of the commentators gives as the reason for this exemption the fact that such cards are not leaflets (*folia*) of indulgences.[33]

The writer fails to see the value of this reasoning or argument, especially since the canon includes the publication of all indulgences, even though they are not printed in leaflets. This reason ought to be abandoned. The other reasons given are sufficient and valid.

CANON 1388 § 2

> § 2. Requiritur vero expressa licentia Sedis Apostolicae ut typis edere liceat, quovis idiomate, tum collectionem authenticam precum piorumque operum quibus Sedes Apostolica indulgentias annexuit, tum elenchum indulgentiarum apostolicarum, tum summarium indulgentiarum vel antea collectum, sed nunquam approbatum, vel nunc primum ex diversis concessionibus colligendum.

A. Development of the Law Enacted in Canon 1388, §2

The law concerning the three works containing special groups of indulgences is intimately connected with the history of the works themselves. Hence, each will be treated in turn: (1) the authentic collection of indulgenced prayers and devotions; (2) the list of apostolic indulgences; (3) the collections which have never been approved by Rome.

---

[32] *DDC*, III, col. 163.

[33] De Meester, *Compendium, loc. cit.;* Marc-Gestermann-Raus, *loc. cit.;* Vermeersch, *De Prohibitione*, n. 87; Beste, *Introductio*, p. 683; Coronata, *Institutiones*, II, n. 956, 2°; Boudinhon, *Nouv. Législ.*, p. 170; Vermeersch-Creusen, *Epitome*, II, n. 725; Hollweck, *Das kirchliche Bücherverbot* (2. ed., Mainz, 1897), p. 36; note 3; Cappello, *De Curia Romana* (2 vols., Romae, 1911–1912), I, 284; Ayrinhac, *Admin. Legisl.*, p. 282; Claeys Bouuaert-Simenon, *Manuale*, III, n. 185; Piscetta-Gennaro, *Elementa*, II, n. 126; Ubach, *Theol. Moral.*, I, 558; Noldin-Schmitt, *Summa*, II, n. 700; *Theologia Mechliniensis: Tractatus de Censuris, Casibus Reservatis, Irregularitatibus, et Libris Prohibitis ad usum alumnorum Seminarii Archiepiscopalis Mechliniensis* (3. ed., Mechliniae, 1906), p. 214, note 1 (hereafter cited as *Theol. Mechlin.*).

(1) THE AUTHENTIC COLLECTIONS OF INDULGENCED PRAYERS AND DEVOTIONS

The Authentic Collection of indulgenced prayers and devotions, better known as the *Raccolta,* was originally published as a private collection by Telesforo Galli, a consultor of the Sacred Congregation of Indulgences. Between the time of its first appearance (1807) and the death of the author (1845) eleven editions had been issued. Aloysius Prinzivalli (*Substitutus* of the same Congregation) published two subsequent editions.

Since the greatest care was taken to include all the known indulgences, and to publish as perfect an edition as possible, the Sacred Congregation approved the thirteenth edition in 1854 (the second of Prinzivalli) as the authentic collection, and the decisive norm for settling any doubts about the issuance of the indulgences contained therein.[34] However, even this edition was not complete. Consequently, the Congregation of Indulgences itself prepared the following edition, published it, and declared it the official collection of authentic indulgences.[35]

From 1877 onward, the Sacred Congregation considered the publication of the official and authentic collection of indulgenced prayers and devotions to be a matter pertaining exclusively to itself. Contemporary decrees of the Sacred Congregation of Indulgences mention in detail the powers of the local ordinaries, but fail to include this one.[36]

Pope Leo XIII failed to make explicit mention of this reservation in his Constitution "*Officiorum ac munerum,*" but it was taken for granted that the phrase "*non publicentur absque competentis auctoritatis licentia*" of article 17 retained the previous law intact. Thus, in fact, the Sacred Congregation of Indulgences declared the law a short time later.[37]

---

[34] Beringer, *Die Ablässe,* I, n. 156; *Decr. Auth. Indulg.,* n. 361.

[35] See the approval of the 1877 edition of the Raccolta, contained in *The Raccolta or Collection of Prayers and Good Works to which the Sovereign Pontiffs have attached Holy Indulgences, published by order of His Holiness, Pope Pius IX* (translation authorized and approved by the Sacred Congregation of Indulgences, Philadelphia, 1881), p. viii (hereafter cited *The Raccolta,* 1877 edition). The decree of approval is dated 3 iun. 1877.

[36] E.g., *Petrocoren.,* 22 ian. 1858—*Decr. Auth. Indulg.,* n. 383.

[37] Decr. 7 aug. 1897—*ASS,* XXX (1897–1898), 175.

The Code mentions the authentic collection of indulgenced prayers and devotions explicitly in canon 1388, § 2.

(2) LISTS OF APOSTOLIC INDULGENCES

There is no earlier law concerning lists of apostolic indulgences. When Pope Leo XIII, Pope Pius X and Pope Benedict XV published their lists of apostolic indulgences, they expressly included a special prohibition in the document of grant:

> Tandem Sanctitas Sua vult et praecipit, praesentem elenchum Indulgentiarum pro maiori fidelium commodo edi typis posse non solum latina lingua vel italica, sed alio quoqumque idiomate, ita tamen ut pro quolibet elencho, qui ubicumque et quovis idiomate edatur, adsit approbatio S. Congregationis Indulgentiarum.[38]

The Code, then, by including the list of Apostolic Indulgences among those works for the printing of which a special permission of the Holy See is required, permanently placed this condition for all future lists of Apostolic Indulgences. For that reason, Popes Pius XI and Pius XII made no mention of a special prohibition when they granted their lists of apostolic indulgences.[39]

(3) COLLECTIONS NOT YET APPROVED BY ROME

The first decree restricting the publication of collections of indulgences not yet approved by the Holy See is relatively early, dating from the pontificate of Pope Innocent XI (1676-1689). It concerned the indulgences of certain confraternities.[40] Pope Bene-

---

[38] For that of Pope Leo XIII cf. S. C. Indulg., 23 febr. 1878—*Rescripta Authentica Sacrae Congregationis Indulgentiis Sacrisque Reliquiis praepositae necnon Summaria Indulgentiarum* (ed. cura J. Schneider, Ratisbonae-Neo Eboraci-Cincinnati, 1885), pp. 345–348 (hereafter cited as *Rescr. Auth.*) ; for that of Pope Pius X, cf. S. C. Indulg., 28 aug. 1903—*ASS*, XXXVI (1903–1904), 125–128; for that of Pope Benedict XV, cf. S. C. S. Off., 5 sept. 1914—*AAS*, VI (1914), 503–506. Due to the reorganization of the Roman Congregations in 1908, the list of Apostolic Indulgences of Benedict XV was issued through the Holy Office.

[39] S. Poenit. Ap., 17 febr. 1922—*AAS*, XIV (1922), 143–144; 11 mart. 1939—*AAS*, XXXI (1939), 132–134.

[40] S. C. Indulg., 7 mart. 1678—*Fontes*, n. 4951; *Decr. Auth. Indulg.*, n. 18.

dict XIV (1740–1758) gave control over the collections of indulgences to the Congregation of Indulgences, without withdrawing the power of the local ordinaries to approve the same collections.[41] The decree of Pope Benedict gave rise to frequent doubts concerning its extension. Therefore the Sacred Congregation settled the question in 1858, the pertinent section of which decree forms the basis for the law concerning the collections of indulgences as that law is now found in canon 1388, § 2:

> E contra vero, si sermo sit de Summario vel antea collecto, sed numquam approbato, vel nunc primum ex diversis concessionibus colligendo, requiritur expressa Sacrae Congregationis Indulgentiarum licentia . . .[42]

This rule was mitigated some years later, so that a bishop was made competent to authorize the publication of summaries of indulgences for societies and confraternities affiliated with an Order or a Congregation, even though the indulgences be drawn from various grants or concessions, and even though the previous decree had forbidden it.[43]

Pope Leo XIII implicitly approved the previous law in article 17 of his Constitution " *Officiorum ac munerum,*" and this was made explicit by a response of the Congregation of Indulgences in that same year.[44]

The Code adopted the previous law concerning the collections of indulgences. It gathered together into § 2 of canon 1388 the three kinds of works for the publication of which it was necessary to obtain permission from the Holy See. The text reads:

> Requiritur vero expressa licentia Sedis Apostolicae ut typis edere liceat, quovis idiomate, tum collectionem authenticam precum piorumque operum quibus Sedes Apostolica indulgentias annexuit, tum elenchum indulgentiarum apostolicarum, tum summarium indulgentiarum

[41] See what was written about this decree in the preceding study of § 1 of canon 1388, *supra.*

[42] *Petrocoren.,* 22 ian. 1858—*Decr. Auth. Indulg.,* n. 383.

[43] S. C. Indulg., *Urbis et Orbis,* 8 ian. 1861—*Decr. Auth. Indulg.,* n. 388; *Fontes,* n. 5061.

[44] Decr. 7 aug. 1897—*ASS,* XXX (1897–1898), 195.

vel antea collectum, sed nunquam approbatum, vel nunc primum ex diversis concessionibus colligendum.

B. Commentary

The commentary on the second paragraph of canon 1388 will be divided as follows: (1) the matter to be submitted; (2) translations; (3) the competent authority and censorship; (4) approval; (5) exceptions; (6) prohibition; (7) summary.

(1) THE MATTER SUBJECT TO THIS CANON

Canon 1388, § 2, reserves three kinds of works for the special permission of the Holy See: (a) the authentic collection of indulgenced prayers and devotions; (b) the list of apostolic indulgences; (c) any new collection of indulgences.

(a) The first kind of work is the authentic collection of indulgenced prayers and devotions, better known as the *Raccolta.* The Raccolta contains all the general indulgences recognized by the Church, i.e., all those indulgences which can be gained at any time by all the faithful, or by groups of the faithful, anywhere in the world.[45] Save for the editing of translations and duplicate editions, which will be discussed later, the publication of the *Raccolta* is reserved exclusively to the Holy See. The material of this collection can no longer be augmented, decreased or altered by any private individual. It is the official and authentic collection published in the name of the Sacred Penitentiary.

(b) The second kind of work reserved to the Holy See is the list of apostolic indulgences, i.e., those which a Pope issues at the beginning of his Pontificate. Although this list is published anew by each successive Pontiff, the list retains a basic similarity. However, no standard list can be given, simply because it remains the option of the Holy Father to grant any indulgences he chooses.

---

[45] *Preces et Pia Opera in favorem omnium Christifidelium vel quorumdam coetuum personarum indulgentiis ditata et opportune recognita* (Civitate Vaticana: Typis Polyglottis Vaticanis, 1938), p. vii (hereafter cited as *Preces et Pia Opera*). There is also an appendix containing indulgences attaching to a visit to certain pious places in Rome. All subsequent references to the Raccolta will be taken from this [1938] edition, unless otherwise indicated.

The current list, granted by Pope Pius XII several days after his accession to the throne of Peter, is fairly representative.[46]

(c) The third kind of work reserved to the Holy See is any new collection of indulgences. A collection is a more or less complete group of indulgences arranged in some definite order, e.g. chronological or systematic. The actual size of the collection, as well as the number of indulgences included, seems to be immaterial as long as the notion of a summary is verified. However, the term does not include the publication of one indulgence, or even of several indulgences in a leaflet, a paper, a prayerbook, a periodical, a textbook, etc., even though the book contains a commentary on the indulgences. The work must be a collection of indulgences *ex professo*.[47] A collection, for example, could comprise the indulgences requiring the use of a specially blessed object, or the indulgences enjoining a visit to a particular church or shrine, or those demanding inscription in certain societies, etc.[48] Such collections are not only possible, but even desirable.[49]

Actually, the text of the canon makes a distinction between two different collections of indulgences—those already in existence, and those yet to be made. It is immediately evident why the Code should reserve to the Holy See the granting of permission for all new collections. But it is less apparent why collections already in existence should have been mentioned, i.e., those which never received the permission of the Holy See. Commentators fail to mention a single example of such a collection, and efforts to dis-

[46] S. Poenit. Ap., 11 mart. 1939—*AAS,* XXXI (1939), 132–134.

[47] Numerous indulgences are mentioned in Cardinal Lepicier's *Indulgences, Their Origin, Nature and Development* (3. ed., London: Burns Oates and Washbourne Ltd., 1928), and yet the book bears only the *Imprimatur* of the Bishop. It is not *ex professo* a collection of Indulgences.

[48] *Preces et Pia Opera* (p. vii) mentions these classes as not contained in the *Raccolta.*

[49] On the occasion of the publication of the 1928 edition of the *Raccolta,* Vermeersch wrote: "Nascitur humile votum ut etiam de anterioribus indulgentiis, de quibus tot sunt dubia, similis collectio mox promulgetur. Ita, v.g. quam multa incerta de indulgentiis usitatissimae viae crucis."—"Annotationes"—*Periodica de Religiosis et Missionariis,* Brugis, 1905–1919; *Periodica de Re Canonica et Morali utili praesertim Religiosis et Missionariis,* Brugis, 1920–1927; *Periodica de Re Morali, Canonica, Liturgica,* Brugis, 1927–1936; Romae, 1937—), XVIII (1929), 171.

cover one have proved fruitless. As far as the writer could ascertain, all collections of indulgences published in modern times have received the requisite permission. There are three [50] collections of indulgences, namely that of Beringer (1838–1909)-Steinen,[51] of Mocchegiani (1839–1905) [52] and of Maurel (+ 1874).[53]

Some light is brought to the problem through an examination of the text in its historical development. The text of canon 1388, § 2, is taken verbatim, in fact almost literally, from a decree of 1858:

> Si sermo sit de Summario vel antea collecto, sed numquam approbato, vel nunc primum ex diversis concessionibus colligendo, requiritur expressa Sacrae Congregationis Indulgentiarum licentia.[54]

The Congregation primarily gave its decision in order to settle a doubt about the extension of the episcopal authority, and only by way of contrast did it mention the extent of the authority of the Holy See. The doubt and the solution were kept on an academic plane. There was no reference to the danger, either proximate or remote, that an older collection might be republished. Older collections must have appeared without the permission of the Holy See in previous centuries, but from the time of the Council of Trent until Leo XIII such collections were automatically designated as prohibited collections.[55] Today such collections may have a historical, a canonical or a liturgical value in themselves, but there would be little practical reason to republish them.

As a consequence, commentators are at a loss to explain the

---

[50] Collections of indulgences are not to be identified with collections of the decrees of the Sacred Congregation of Indulgences. The well-known collections of Prinzivalli, Falise (+ 1881), Schneider (+ 1884), etc., which belong to this latter class, will be treated under canon 1389, together with the Collections of the Roman Congregations.

[51] *Die Ablässe.*

[52] *Collectio Indulgentiarum theologice, canonice ac historice digesta* (Quaracchi, 1897).

[53] *Die Ablässe, ihr Wesen und ihr Gebrauch* (Paderborn, 1860).

[54] S. C. Indulg., *Petrocoren.*, 22 ian. 1858—*Decr. Auth. Indulg.*, n. 383; *Fontes*, n. 5059.

[55] Pennacchi (*ASS*, XXX [1897–1898], 328–334) wrote extensively on the older law, and why and how it was abrogated by Leo XIII.

present text of the Code. Some merely repeat the law as it stands and decline to offer comment. Practically all the rest simply state that the present law applies to new collections alone.[56] Other commentators express the thought somewhat differently, but with the same practical result. They claim that only the first edition is reserved to the Holy See.[57]

This interpretation is entirely in conformity with the pre-Code law, for the decree of 1858 from which canon 1388, § 2 is derived has the following passage as well:

> Si agatur de edenda concessione alicuius indulgentiae, vel Summarii indulgentiarum, quod ex Brevi Apostolico, vel Rescripto desumendum est, aut de Summario ex auctoritate Sacrae Congregationis iam vulgato, in potestate Ordinarii sit licentiam concedere earumdem indulgentiarum concessiones typis imprimendi (dummodo pro aliquo elencho non sit specialis et expressa prohibitio).[58]

Similarly, this interpretation seems in perfect conformity with the present law, for the Code reserves any collection, either old or new, which has not yet received the permission of the Holy See. Hence, it seems permissible to hold that the present law reserves only new collections to the Holy See.

(2) TRANSLATIONS

A special question arises from the inclusion of "*quovis idiomate*" in the text of the canon. The Holy See reserves to itself the granting of permission for any of these three kinds of collections, in whatever language they may appear. However, as mentioned

---

[56] This opinion is not new. It was held even before the Code, e.g., by Vermeersch, *De Prohibitione*, n. 87; Cappello, *De Curia Romana*, I, 283–284; Commentators writing after the promulgation of the Code are Augustine, *Commentary*, IV, 374; Haring, *Grundzüge des katholischen Kirchenrechts* (2. ed., 2 vols., Graz, 1924), I, 372–373; Wernz-Vidal, *Ius Canonicum*, IV, pars 2, n. 711; Sipos *Enchiridion*, p. 713, note 16; Gagnon, *La Censure*, n. 224; Coronata, *Institutiones*, II, n. 956, 2°, with hesitancy.

[57] Pejška, *Ius Canonicum*, p. 171; Tummulo-Iorio, *De Censuris*, n. 1022, note 2; Vermeersch-Creusen, *Epitome*, II, n. 726, 3°.

[58] S. C. Indulg., *Petrocoren.*, 22 ian. 1858—*Decr. Auth. Indulg.*, n. 383; *Fontes*, n. 5059.

above, this permission applies only to the first edition of a translation in any language.[59]

In granting permission for the translation of a collection of indulgences, the Holy See is not quite as severe, apparently, as for the permission of the original edition. Perhaps it is felt that once the original work has been censored and adjudged as meeting all the requirements, a translation can more easily meet these requirements. For that reason, it seems, the Sacred Penitentiary may permit the translation and censorship to be carried out under the care of the local ordinary. In such a case, the Sacred Penitentiary grants a conditional permission which becomes effective when the local ordinary testifies that the censorship has been favorable.[60] Such, in fact, was the procedure for the recent English translation of the *Raccolta.* Cardinal (then Archbishop) Spellman had petitioned the Holy See for permission to translate the Raccolta, and the Sacred Penitentiary granted permission in 1941:

> Sacra Paenitentiaria Apostolica, vi facultatum a Ssmo D. N. Pio Pp. XII sibi tributarum, benigne annuit pro gratia iuxta preces, dummodo Excmo Oratori de fidelitate versionis constet.[61]

The *Imprimatur* was given by Archbishop Spellman more than two years later, Dec. 8, 1943.[62]

---

[59] Jombart, *DDC*, III, col. 163.

[60] If Dr. Breen obtained permission to publish his translation of the Raccolta (*A Collection of Indulgenced Prayers to which the Supreme Roman Pontiffs for all Christians or for definite organizations of persons have attached indulgences from the year 1899 to the year 1928,* Milwaukee: Keystone, Inc., 1931) there is no record of it in the book. There is an *Imprimatur,* and also a letter from Card. Lepicier, from which the following is taken: "As soon as your manuscript was in my hands, I made enquiries at the Sacred Penitentiary, even as you directed, but I was told that it is not the custom of that Sacred Tribunal to issue formal approbation of new translations of indulgences, and that they consider as sufficient the Ordinary's approval, according to canon law." Perhaps Dr. Breen thought this was sufficient.

[61] S. Poenit. Ap., 14 iun. 1941—*The Raccolta* or *Prayers and Devotions enriched with indulgences authorized by the Holy See* (New York: Benziger Bros., 1943), p. iv.

[62] *Ibid.,* p. v.

A possible difficulty could arise from the careless reading of canon 934, § 2, in comparison with canon 1388, § 2. The former reads:

> Si pecularis oratio assignata fuerit, indulgentiae acquiri possunt quocumque idiomate oratio recitetur, dummodo de fidelitate versionis constet ex declaratione vel Sacrae Poenitentiariae vel unius ex Ordinariis loci ubi vulgaris est lingua in quam vertitur oratio.

As the text clearly indicates, canon 934, § 2, is dealing only with individual prayers (*peculiaris oratio*), while canon 1388, § 2, treats of collections of indulgences. Furthermore, canon 934, § 2, is not concerned primarily with the publication of these indulgences, but with their translation. As was seen above, the Holy See is satisfied with a translation of a whole collection, as long as it is approved by a local ordinary.

For a second edition of a translation of a collection of indulgences, the permission of the Holy See is not required. However, one thing must be remembered. Each edition of the *Raccolta* is a work wholly independent of the former edition when published by the authority and in the name of the Holy See. It abrogates all previous editions. Translations must always be made from the latest Vatican edition.

(3) THE COMPETENT AUTHORITY AND CENSORSHIP

Canon 1388, § 2, reserves the permission for the publication of these three kinds of collections to the Holy See. The Code elsewhere, in canon 258, § 2, assigns the jurisdiction over indulgences (save in doctrinal matters) to the exclusive competency of the Sacred Penitentiary. Hence, in virtue of canon 7, the term Holy See must here be understood to mean the Sacred Penitentiary.

According to the general rule, censorship belongs to the authority to whom the permission for the publication is reserved. Hence, for the publication of any of these three collections, the permission and the censorship of the Sacred Penitentiary must precede. Ordinarily the Sacred Penitentiary is extremely meticulous in performing the censorship, and in stating the accomplishment of the act when the approval is given. For example, the approval given to Beringer-Steinen may be cited:

> Cum Sacra Poenitentiaria Apostolica editionem Operis quod inscribitur "Franz Beringer. *Die Ablässe, ihr Wesen und Gebrauch.* Nach den neuesten Entscheidungen und Bewilligungen bearbeitet von Pet. Al. Steinen, S.I. I Bd. 15. Auflage. Paderborn, 1920, Ferd. Schöningh," uni ex suis consultoribus examinandum dederit, qui maturo praefati Operis examine peracto testatus est illam Decretis et Concessionibus Apostolicae Sedis in materia Indulgentiarum invenisse undequaque conformem ideoque Indulgentias inibi relatas esse authenticas et preces insertas in germanicam linguam fideliter esse translatas, attento praedicto testimonio, eadem Sacra Poenitentiaria Apostolica hanc primi voluminis editionem typis imprimi ac publicari benigne permisit.
>
> (Sig.) O. Card. Giorgi, Poen. Mai.
> " Fr. Borgongini Duca, Secret.[63]

From the document one can conclude that the Sacred Penitentiary is interested in several special features of censorship, namely, to discover the presence or absence of false or apocryphal indulgences,[64] the conformity of the present edition with the official edition, and the fidelity of the translation.[65] For the rest, the cen-

---

[63] S. Poenit. Ap., apr. 30, 1920—Beringer-Steinen, *op. cit.,* p. ii. It is interesting to observe that in the second volume there is the approbation of the Sacred Penitentiary March 5, 1916, and the *Imprimi potest* of the religious Superior; while the first volume bears the *Imprimatur* of the Bishop [actually of the Vicar General] dated March 14, 1919, the *Imprimi potest* of the religious Superior, and the approbation of the Sacred Penitentiary, dated April 30, 1920. One could perhaps conclude that the Sacred Penitentiary required the matter to be subjected first to the local ordinary for the usual censorship, and only then examined the same work "*in materia indulgentiarum.*" This manner of procedure, however, is not indicated by the Code, and hence cannot be considered as necessary.

[64] Canon 1399, 11°, states that books, in which apocryphal indulgences, or those proscribed or revoked by the Church, are contained are *ipso facto* prohibited books.

[65] Canon 934, § 2, states that any addition, subtraction or interpolation of the indulgenced prayer occasions for it the loss of the indulgence. The Holy See clarified this statement by adding that only a substantial change in the prayer would occasion this loss. Cf. S. Poenit. Ap., 26 nov. 1934—*AAS,* XXVI (1934), 643.

sorship follows the general rules of the first paragraph of canon 1388. When the Sacred Penitentiary examines an indulgence, however, it has the opportunity of comparing it with the original grant, the document of which is kept in the archives. Hence, an approval by the Sacred Penitentiary is always the most reliable form of censorship that can be had.

(4) APPROVAL

The permission to print a collection of indulgences is not the same thing as the approval of that collection. This is particularly evident when the Holy See gives the permission and the local ordinary grants the approval. When the Holy See approves a collection, it may do so in one of several different ways, each of which implies a different degree of approval.

(a) *Simple approval* is given when the authority gives the *Imprimatur*. When this alone is given, it means that the censorship has been performed, the censor has given his *nihil obstat,* and there is nothing objectionable in the collection. This is the lowest grade of approval.

(b) *Approval of the text* guarantees that the text is genuine. The value of this approval is apparent, for it happens that copies of the original are not always as faithful as is desired. Variant readings may be in circulation. The decisive text is the one to which the Holy See has given this special approval, and to it all others must cede. The *Raccolta* gained this type of approval very early. Such approval is clearly evident in the 1831 edition:

> Eadem Sacra Congregatio praelaudatum Opus haud dubie perutile probat, ac uti authenticum publicari posse censet. Monet tamen, quod si in quacumque eiusdem Operis editione, seu versione cuiuscumque idiomatis tam in Urbe, quam extra exarata, vel quae exarari contingat, dubium aliquod subinde emerserit sive quoad Indulgentiarum concessiones, sive quoad praescriptas conditiones adimplendas, *ad praesentem tantum Romanam Editionem hoc Anno Millesimo Octingentesimo Trigesimo Primo typis Perego-Salvioni gnaviter excusam, et in ipsius S. Congregationis Secretaria asservatam recursus habeatur.*[66]

---

[66] S. C. Indulg., 30 apr. 1831—*Raccolta di Orazioni e Pie Opere per le quali sono state concedute dai Sommi Pontefici le S. Indulgenze* (7. ed.,

The approval of the text does not alter the nature of the work as such. The *Raccolta* still remained the work of a private individual until 1877, even though the text was standardized and approved by the Holy See as early as 1831.

(c) *Approval of the collection as official* withdraws the collection from the ranks of all private works, and makes it the official publication of the Sacred Congregation of Indulgences. As was mentioned above, the *Raccolta* became the official collection in 1877. Beringer-Steinen's collection has received approval from the Holy See, but still it is not designated as the official collection. The individual indulgences in an official collection remain just as they were before the official approval. The only difference lies in the fact that the Holy See takes upon itself the responsibility for the entire collection in a new way, e.g., as in the approval of the 1877 edition of the *Raccolta:*

> Hanc ergo *Collectionem,* iuxta Sanctitatis Suae mandatum, rite accurateque absolutam, typisque S. Congregationis de *Propaganda Fide* editam, SS. D. N. Pius Papa IX apostolica sua auctoritate approbavit.[67]

(d) *Approval as official and extended to all the faithful* means that each and every indulgence contained in the collection is valid for all the faithful. Even though any of the indulgences contained therein had been particular indulgences before, they now become general or universal. Evidently, the *Raccolta* gained this distinction in 1877, when it became both official and universal.[68]

(e) *Approval as official and universal and exclusive* means that the collection thus approved contains each and every general indulgence recognized by the Church at the time of that edition.

Romae: Typografia Perego-Salvioni, 1831), pp. 464–465. The italics are in the original. This was the earliest edition available to the writer. Similar prescriptions are found in subsequent editions, for example, in the thirteenth edition: S. C. Indulg., 15 dec. 1854, in Falise, *Sacrae Congregationis Indulgentiarum Resolutiones Authenticae* (Lovanii, 1862), p. 29.

[67] S. C. Indulg., 3 iun. 1877—*The Raccolta* [1877 edition], p. x.

[68] The basis for all these distinctions is taken from Cicognani, *Canon Law* ([tr. O'Hara-Brennan] Philadelphia: The Dolphin Press, 1934), pp. 132–134. These distinctions are there applied to Collections of Laws, but they are adaptable to Collections of Indulgences as well.

Subsequent editions may be official, universal and exclusive. In as far as they omit any general indulgence contained in former collections, they abrogate them. The *Raccolta* alone, of all the collections of indulgences, enjoys this unique distinction. It obtained this exclusiveness as early as 1877:

> SS. D. N. Pius Papa IX apostolica sua auctoritate approbavit; praeceptique a cunctis Christifidelibus, ut genuinam et authenticam Indulgentiarum hactenus concessarum Syllogen prorsus habendum esse.[69]

It is interesting to observe the singular manner in which the decree of approval for the 1928 edition of the Raccolta reads:

> Ssmus D. N. Pius divina Providentia Pp. XI Collectionem hanc typis vaticanis impressam, approbavit et confirmavit, et abrogatis generalibus indulgentiarum concessionibus post dictum annum [1898, the year of the latest previous edition of the Raccolta] factis, in eadem Collectione non relatis, ipsam tantum uti authenticam haberi mandavit.[70]

The decree approving the 1938 edition repeated the same formula, but struck out the words "*post dictum annum factis,*" thus making the text read "*abrogatis generalibus indulgentiarum concessionibus in eadem Collectione non relatis,*"[71] and thus restored the exclusiveness of the newly edited collection to its absolute character.

(5) THE EXCEPTION

Throughout the history of the collections of indulgences, there appeared the practice of allowing one special collection of indulgences—namely, a collection prepared by an Order, Institute or Archconfraternity for a Society which it aggregates to be printed without the permission of the Holy See. This exemption is not mentioned in the Code, but neither is it revoked. When the general rule of the reservation of all collections to the Holy See was made in 1858, it was doubtful whether the exemption still

---

[69] *The Raccolta* or *Collection of Prayers and Good Works* [1881], p. x.
[70] S. Poenit. Ap., 22 febr. 1929—*AAS,* XXI (1929), 200.
[71] S. Poenit. Ap., 31 dec. 1937—*AAS,* XXX (1938), 111.

held, but in a specific decree of the Congregation of Indulgences it was upheld:

> Et ut Societati aggregatae ab Ordine, Instituto, seu Archiconfraternitate aggregante tradi possit separatim et distincte a formula ac etiam typis impressus elenchus indulgentiarum et privilegiorum ab Ordinario tamen loci recognitus; cuius impressio in hunc tantum finem permittitur, etiamsi indulgentiarum concessiones sint depromptae ex pluribus Brevibus, etc., non obstante decreto S. C. Indicis et altero decreto Sacrae Congregationis Indulgentiarum explicante et moderante decretum Indicis diei 22 Ianuarii 1858.[72]

This exemption is generally allowed by commentators after the Code as well.[73]

(6) PROHIBITION

A collection of indulgences published without the required permission is not a prohibited work for that reason alone. However, such a work is always suspect. Similarly, a work published without the observance of the conditions imposed by the Holy See when it grants the permission is not a prohibited work, unless it contains false or apocryphal indulgences (canon 1399, 11°). Canon 934, § 2, states that additions, omissions, or alterations in the text of an indulgenced prayer occasion for the prayer the loss of the indulgence. This was explained by the Holy See as applying only to substantial changes,[74] and not to the errors incidental to printing, as long as there have not resulted any serious alterations in the form or the doctrine. Books which contain such errors, as well as those which fail to have the requisite permission, may be used by the faithful.[75]

---

[72] S. C. Indulg., 8 ian. 1861—*Decr. Auth. Indulg.*, n. 388.

[73] De Meester, *Compendium,* III, pars 1, n. 1345; Vermeersch-Creusen, Epitome, II, n. 725; Wernz-Vidal, *Ius Canonicum,* IV, pars 2, n. 711 (22); Blat, *Commentarium,* III, pars 2, n. 276; Augustine, *Commentary,* IV, 374; Beste, *Introductio,* p. 683; Coronata, *Institutiones,* II, n. 956, 2°; Beringer-Steinen, *Die Ablässe,* I, 209; Boudinhon, *Nouv. Législ.,* p. 168, note 1; Vermeersch, *De Prohibitione,* n. 87; Gagnon, *La Censure,* n. 225; Cappello, *De Curia Romana,* I, 284.

[74] S. Poenit. Ap., 26 nov. 1934—*AAS,* XXVI (1934), 643.

[75] Gennari, *Monit. Eccl.,* X, pars 1 (1897), 67; Wernz-Vidal, *Ius Cano-*

(7) SUMMARY

Canon 1388, § 1, requires the permission of the local ordinary for the publication of all indulgences, except the publication of those which are reserved to the Holy See by canon 1388, §2. The list given in the canon is not an all-inclusive list. The local ordinary, i.e., any of the three mentioned in canon 1385, § 2, is the competent authority to grant the permission, and also to perform the censorship. The censor must assure himself of the conformity of the proposed indulgence with the authentic grant, either by comparing it with the original document, or with an authentic copy thereof. The printing of indulgenced prayers or ejaculations on cards for private distribution at some religious occasion is allowed, even without the permission of the local ordinary. Canon 1388, § 1, is merely a restatement of canon 1385, § 1, and is inserted among the group of reserved publications for the sake of introducing the indulgences which are reserved to the Holy See and, by way of contrast, of making the law better understood.

Canon 1388, § 2, reserves the publication of three special kinds of works to the permission of the Holy See: (1) the authentic collection of indulgenced prayers and devotions (the *Raccolta*); (2) the list of apostolic indulgences; (3) any new collection of indulgences. The publication of each and every independent translation (i.e., the first edition) of these three kinds of works is also reserved to the permission of the Holy See.

Censorship of these three kinds of works is reserved to the authority to whom the permission for the publication is reserved, i.e., to the Sacred Penitentiary. This censorship investigates the reliability of the indulgences proposed, and the fidelity of the translation. There are five grades of approval which a collection of indulgences may receive: (1) simple permission, i.e., *nihil obstat;* (2) approval of the text; (3) approval of a collection as official; (4) approval of a collection as official and extended to

---

nicum, IV, pars 2, n. 711; Pennacchi, *ASS,* XXX (1897–1898), 146; Gagnon, *La Censure,* n. 299; De Meester, *Compendium,* III, pars 1, n. 1345; *Theol. Mechlin.,* p. 215; Vermeersch, *De Prohibitione,* n. 87; Cappello, *De Curia Romana,* I, 284; Wernz, *Ius Decretalium,* III, pars 1, n. 111 (71). Boudinhon (*Nouv. Législ.,* p. 170) calls this a new type of law which applies only to editors and publishers, but not to readers.

all the faithful; (5) approval as official and universal and exclusive.

There is one collection that may be published apart from the otherwise specially needed recourse to Rome, that is, the collection of indulgences which pertain to a society affiliated with an Order, Institute or Archconfraternity.

A collection published without the permission of Rome is not, for that reason alone, a prohibited collection. Similarly, one published without the observance of the conditions imposed is not a prohibited collection. Both are indeed suspect. But the only collections that are prohibited are those which publish false or apocryphal indulgences. An addition, omission or alteration occasions for the indulgenced prayer the loss of the otherwise attached indulgence if the alteration is substantial.

CHAPTER III

COLLECTIONS OF DECREES OF THE ROMAN CONGREGATIONS

(Canon 1389)

Collectiones decretorum Romanorum Congregationum rursus edi nequeunt, nisi impetrata prius licentia et servatis conditionibus a Moderatoribus uniuscuiusque Congregationis praescriptis.

A. Development of the Law Enacted in Canon 1389

The Roman Congregations are of relatively recent origin in the Church. Some few Congregations can trace their lineage back to the Middle Ages,[1] but none began their existence as Congregations until the time of the Council of Trent. Most of them owe their origin to Pope Sixtus V (1585–1590), who established fifteen Congregations in 1588.[2] At various times the Popes have seen fit to modify the nature, constitution or competency of these Congregations, to increase or decrease their jurisdiction, to establish new Congregations and to abolish the old. The latest complete reorganization was effected by Pope Pius X in his Constitution "*Sapienti consilio.*" [3]

---

[1] Several excellent historical studies of the Roman Congregations exist: Cappello, *De Curia Romana* (2 vols., Romae, 1911–1912); Ojetti, *De Romana Curia* (Romae, 1910); Monin, *De Curia Romana* (Lovanii, 1912); Martin, *The Roman Curia* (New York, 1913). Among the authors who treated of the Roman Curia prior to the time of its reorganization in 1908 by Pope Pius X the reader may profitably consult Bangen, *Die römische Kurie, ihre gegenwärtige Zusammensitzung und ihr Geschäftsgang. Nach mehrjähriger eigener Anschauung dargastellt* (Münster, 1854); Phillips, *Kirchenrecht* (7 vols., Regensburg, 1845–1872), VI, 1–803; Hilling, *Procedure at the Roman Curia.* (A concise and practical handbook, translated and adapted with the author's consent, New York: J. F. Wagner, 1907.)

[2] Const., "*Immensa,*" 22 ian. 1588—*BRT*, VIII, 985–999.

[3] 29 iun. 1908—*AAS*, I (1909), 7–19.

(1) THE DECREE OF 1631

In the course of time the Congregations have issued many decrees, responses and decisions. Some were merely private, but others were of a more general character. A copy of each was kept in the archives of the Congregation, while other copies were sent to the interested parties. There was no official publication wherein a complete list of all the documents could be made available for the public. In fact, some archives were secret archives.

Shortly after the Congregation of the Council began to issue acts and decrees, there began to appear small collections of some of these responses and decisions. In 1621 the Congregation found it necessary to ban some collections on the grounds that they contained inexact renditions of the official documents, that they even included apocryphal documents, and that they were published without the permission of the Congregation. To make this effective, the Congregation of the Council instructed the Congregation of the Index to place such works on the Index of Forbidden Books.[4]

(2) LEGISLATION OF BENEDICT XIV (1740–1758)

When Pope Benedict XIV (1740–1758) revised the Index in 1753, he also issued the *Decreta de Libris Prohibitis nec in Indice nominatim Expressis,* which contains a special paragraph of rules entitled "*Libri Prohibiti,*" the second of which reads:

---

[4] S.C.C., decr. 2 aug. 1631—in Boudinhon, *Nouv. Législ.,* p. 236. The Congregation of the Council could forbid the printing of collections, but it was the proper authority of the Congregation of the Index to penalize the authors or collectors by inscribing their works in the Index. The following examples are pertinent, and may be found under the name of the collector: (1) Jean de Gallemart, *Declarationes cardinalium concilii Tridentini interpretum cum citationibus Joannis Sotealli, et remissionibus Augustini Barbosae;* (2) Gallemart, *Sacri Concilii Tridentini decisiones et declarationes cardinalium ejusdem concilii interpretum, praesertim secundum correctionem Petri de Marzilla* (these two works were placed on the Index by decrees of April 29 and June 6, 1621); (3) Augustinus Barbosa, *Remissiones doctorum, qui varia loca concilii Tridentini incidenter tractarunt* (this was condemned in a decree of June 6, 1621); (4) Barbosa, *Collectanea bullarii aliarumve summorum pontificum constitutionum nec non praecipuorum decisionum quae ab Apostolica Sede, et Sacris Congregationibus ad annum 1633 emanarunt* (this work was prohibited in a decree of January 22, 1642).

> Declarationes, decisiones, interpretationes Congregationis concilii Tridentini, earumque collectiones tam impressae, quam imprimendae, ementito ipsius Congregationis nomine.[5]

The Sacred Congregation of Rites is the only other Congregation to have prohibited the publication of its decrees without its permission:

> In hac Congregatione fuit decretum, quod in futurum non liceat imprimere decreta emanata per hanc Sacram Congregationem sine licentia eiusdem Congregationis in scriptis obtinenda, sub poena ducatorum centum auri de Camera, ipso iure per impressores incurrenda. Quod si in aliis operibus iam impressis reperiantur allegata decreta huius Sacrae Congregationis, nulla fides eis adhibeatur, nisi fuerint subscripta a Secretario dictae Congregationis.[6]

When the same Congregation gave permission for the third edition of Gardellini's *Decreta Authentica,* in 1856, it renewed the foregoing decree.[7]

(3) LEGISLATION OF LEO XIII (1878–1903)

Pope Leo XIII (1878–1903), in his Constitution "*Officiorum ac munerum,*" reorganized the question of the censorship and prohibition of books. He adopted the tenor of the decrees pertinent to these two Congregations, and made it applicable to all the Congregations for the future:

> Idem dicendum de Collectionibus Decretorum singularum Romanarum Congregationum; hae nimirum Collectiones edi nequeunt, nisi obtenta prius licentia, et servatis conditionibus a moderatoribus uniuscuiusque Congregationis praescriptis.[8]

---

[5] Cf. *Index Leonis XIII*, p. XXXI, § 2, n. 3.

[6] S. R. C., decr. 14 febr. 1632—*Decr. Auth.,* I, v.

[7] S. R. C., 16 febr. 1856—*Decr. Auth.,* I, v. The work of editing was undertaken by Capalti. Gardellini had died in 1829.

[8] 25. ian. 1897, n. 33—*Fontes,* n. 632.

(4) CANON 1389

Canon 1389 adopts this law almost verbatim. The word "*rursus*" is added before "*edi nequeunt*":

> Collectiones decretorum Romanarum Congregationum rursus edi nequeunt, nisi impetrata prius licentia et servatis conditionibus a Moderatoribus uniuscuiusque Congregationis praescriptis.

B. COMMENTARY

Canon 1389 states that collections of decrees of the Roman Congregations may not be re-published unless there first be obtained the permission, and unless likewise there be observed the conditions prescribed by the moderators of the respective Congregations. The commentary on this canon will be divided as follows: (1) The matter subject to this canon; (2) the competent authority and the permission; (3) the censorship and approval; (4) the term *rursus;* (5) summary.

(1) THE MATTER SUBJECT TO THIS CANON

Canon 1389 reveals very plainly that it is concerned with collections of the decrees of the Roman Congregations. It makes no distinction between official collections and private collections, nor between decrees properly so called and the private responses of the Congregations. Hence, the canon incudes all collections of all decrees, regardless of the form in which the collection or the decrees happen to be issued. A collection, in a broad sense, is any accumulation of decrees; but in the strict sense of the canon, it is an ordered assemblage of a mass of decrees.[9]

The definition indicates a material and a formal element in every collection. The material element consists in the mass of decrees.[10]

[9] Vermeersch-Creusen, *Epitome,* II, n. 725; Piat, *NRT,* XXXII (1900), 11; Jombart, *DDC,* III, col. 163.

[10] The material element of a collection must be exclusively understood of the decrees or acts of the Congregation. It is not to be understood as comprising also historical data as contained, for example, in Shearer, *Pontificia Americana: A Documentary History of the Catholic Church in the United States (1784–1884)*, The Catholic University of America Studies in American Church History, Vol. XV (Washington, D. C.: The Catholic University of America, 1933).

This need not be very large, for some Congregations, particularly those of recent origin, have issued relatively few decrees. However, the collection must be more or less complete, according to the purpose of the collector, and the scope of the collection.[11] It is quite immaterial whether the decrees are gathered from one or from several Roman Congregations.[12] Most collections represent one Congregation. The *Fontes,* published by Cardinals Gasparri (1852–1934) and Serédi (1884–1945), represent all Congregations.[13]

The formal element of a collection consists in the ordered arrangement of the decrees. Decrees are usually gathered in the order of their appearance, i.e., in a chronological arrangement, or in the order of their content, i.e., in a topical or systematic arrangement.[14]

Canon 1389 points exclusively to collections of the decrees of the Roman Congregations. No reference is made to collections of the acts of the Roman Tribunals, e.g., the Decisions of the Roman Rota, the mandates or edicts of the Sacred Penitentiary, etc., or to collections of the replies of the Pontifical Commissions established in Rome, e.g., the Pontifical Commission for the Authentic Interpretation of the Code, or the Pontifical Biblical Commission, or to collections of the ordinances of any other ecclesiastical agency in Rome.[15] Hence, the publication of collections of the acts of these other Roman agencies is not governed by canon 1389. For the most part it is governed by the ordinary rules of censorship.[16]

[11] Génnari, *Monit. Eccl.,* X, pars 1 (1897), 107.

[12] Blat, *Commentarium,* III, pars 2, n. 277; Gagnon, *La Censure,* n. 227.

[13] Berutti (*Institutiones,* IV, 430) observes: "Absque praefata [Cardinalis Praefecti vel Cardinalis Secretarii] licentia merito edita sunt volumina IV–VIII *Fontium Codicis Iuris Canonici,* in quibus quamplura—non omnia—Sacrarum Congregationum decreta referuntur, et saepius in illorum tantum parte dispositiva."

[14] Gagnon, *La Censure,* n. 227.

[15] Coronata, *Institutiones,* II, n. 956, 3º; Blat, *Commentarium,* III, pars 2, n. 277; Pennacchi, *ASS,* XXX (1897–1898), 484.

[16] Although canon 1389 governs the publication of a collection of the decrees of the Sacred Congregation of the Council, it has no reference to the publication of a collection of the decrees of a *council.* For example, the decrees of the Council of Trent have been collected and published many times. There was, and still is, a special law governing the republication of

Certain publications give the appearance of being collections of the decrees of the Roman Congregations, whereas in reality they are not. Thus, periodicals and newspapers often reprint or translate the current decrees of the Roman Congregations. The decrees thus reprinted are not of the nature of a collection, even though the periodicals and newspapers follow a policy of recording the complete decrees of all the Congregations as they are issued.[17] Similarly, commentaries, textbooks, dissertations, theses, studies, etc., of Canon Law, Theology, Liturgy, etc., often amass many decrees in support of their text. The authors cite and quote as much as is necessary for a complete understanding of the matter and of their opinions. These works cannot be classed as collections.[18]

Finally, there are certain collections of decrees gathered from the various Roman Congregations, Tribunals, Pontifical Commissions, etc. These works are intended to spread the knowledge of recent decisions. They gather into one place the numerous decrees spread over many volumes of the *Acta Apostolicae Sedis* or traceable even to private sources. Most of these works are ex-

---

the decrees of the Council of Trent. Thus, a decree of the Sacred Congregation of the Council dated July 2, 1629, which forbade the translation of the decrees of the Council of Trent without the special permission of the said Congregation, seems to obtain even today. Cf. *Collectanea Sacrae Congregationis de Propaganda Fide* (Romae, 1893), n. 1867; Piat, *NRT,* XXXII (1900), 17; Pennacchi, *ASS,* XXX (1897-1898), 484-485; Boudinhon, *Nouv. Législ.*, p. 240.

Canon 1389 does not govern the reprinting of the Code of Canon Law, although the law which forbids the republication of the Code without the permission of the Holy See is very similar to the law enacted in canon 1389. The obverse side of the title page in every edition of the Code contains this text: "Nemini liceat sine venia Sanctae Sedis hunc Codicem denuo imprimere aut in aliam linguam vertere."

[17] Piat, *NRT,* XXXII (1900), 12; Woywod, *Commentary,* II, n. 1404; Jombart, *DDC,* III, col. 163.

[18] Piat, *NRT,* XXXII (1900), 12; Pennacchi, *ASS,* XXX (1897-1898), 484; Boudinhon, "Les Nouvelles Règles sur l'Interdiction et la Censure des Livres"—*Le Canoniste Contemporaine* (Paris, 1878—), XXI (1898), 136 hereafter cited as *CC*); Génnari, *Monit. Eccl.,* X, pars I (1897), 107; Vermeersch, *De Prohibitione,* n. 108; Cappello, *De Curia Romana,* I, 293; De Meester, *Compendium,* III, pars 1, n. 1346; Schneider, *Büchergesetze,* p. 122; Beste, *Introductio,* p. 683; Gagnon, *La Censure,* n. 288.

tremely summary in their presentation of the decrees; furthermore, the documents employed are seldom printed in their complete text. The vernacular is often used instead of the original. Hence, it is quite well accepted that these collections are not collections in the strict sense of canon 1389.[19]

All of these have appeared since the Code, and are published with the *Imprimatur* and censorship of the local ordinary. The best known of these collections are Bouscaren, *The Canon Law Digest* (2 vols., Milwaukee: Bruce Publ. Co., 1934–1943); Coronata, *Interpretatio Authentica Codicis Iuris Canonici et circa ipsum Sanctae Sedis Iurisprudentia 1916–1940* (Taurini-Romae: Marietti, 1940); Sartori, *Enchiridion canonicum seu Sanctae Sedis responsiones post editum Codicem Iuris Canonici datae iuxta canonum Codicis ordinem digestae notulisque ornatae (1917–1944)* (7. ed., Romae: Ex Typographia Augustiniana, 1944); Woywod, *Canonical Decisions of the Holy See* (New York: J. Wagner, 1933).[20]

(2) THE COMPETENT AUTHORITY AND THE PERMISSION

The canon places the authority for granting the permission to publish collections of the decrees of the Roman Congregations in the Moderators of the respective Congregations. The Moderator is the Cardinal Prefect or Cardinal Secretary with his advisers.[21]

---

[19] Blat, *Commentarium,* III, pars 2, n. 277; Wernz-Vidal, *Ius Canonicum,* IV, pars 2, n. 711; Gagnon, *La Censure,* n. 228.

[20] Coronata lists the following other collections in the introduction to his own *Interpretatio Authentica,* pp. vii–viii. Bruno, *Codicis Iuris Canonici Interpretationes Authenticae seu Responsa a Pontificia Commissione ad Codicis canones authentice interpretandos annis MCMXVII–MCMXXXV data* (Romae, 1935); Cimetier, *Pour étudier le Code de droit Canonique, Introduction générale. Bibliographie, reponses et décisions. Document complémentaire* 1917–1927 (Paris, 1927) *Supplément* I (1931), *Supplément* II (1938); Hilling, *Codicis Iuris Canonici Interpretatio. Responsiones Sanctae Sedis Codicem Iuris Canonici Illustrantes* (Friburgi Brisigavorum, 1925); Toso, *Repertorium iuridicum ecclesiasticum seu Pontificiae Commissionis Codiciiuris can. interpretando praepositae, responsiones authenticae itemque Curiae Romanae iurisprudentis universa, post editum Codicem publici iuris factum,* I (Romae, 1925); II (Romae, 1931).

[21] Coronata, *Institutiones,* II, n. 956, 3º; Blat, *Commentarium,* III, pars 2, n. 277; Berutti, *Institutiones,* IV, 430.

Each Congregation enjoys exclusive competence over its own acts and decrees, and the permission granted by one Moderator does not extend to the decrees of another Congregation.[22]

Blat maintains that canon 1389 points to the collections of all Roman Congregations, even those which formerly existed but are now suppressed.[23] One will readily admit that the canon is concerned primarily with the republication of existing collections, but it is not so evident that the canon abstracts altogether from the fact of the existence of the Congregation in the present. Rather, the first impression seems to be that the canon is concerned only with the existing Congregations, for it states quite simply the need of first obtaining the permission of the Congregation. Now, it is surely impossible to obtain this permission from a suppressed Congregation. Perhaps Blat simply implies that the permission must be sought from the Congregation which supplanted the suppressed Congregation. Thus, to re-publish the *Index of Forbidden Books,* formerly issued by the Congregation of the Index, one would now seek the permission of the Congregation of the Holy Office. Similarly, to republish the collection of the former Congregation of Immunity, one would now approach the Congregation of the Council. This seems entirely logical and consistent.

However, difficulties would arise. The *Decreta Authentica,* issued formerly by the Congregation of Indulgences, no longer relate to any of the Congregations. All matters concerning indulgences are now handled by one of the Roman Tribunals, the Sacred Penitentiary. Would it be necessary to obtain the permission of the Sacred Penitentiary, even though the Roman

[22] Piat, *NRT,* XXXII (1900), 12; Boudinhon, *CC,* XXI (1898), 135; Pennacchi, *ASS,* XXX (1897–1898), 484; Baart, *Legal Formulary* (5. ed., New York, 1898), n. 271; Woywod, *HPR,* XXVIII (1928), 966; Jombart, *DDC,* III, col. 163; Gagnon, *La Censure,* n. 227. Gagnon, in the place cited, writes that the published collection would have to draw upon the decrees of any one of the Roman Congregations in particular, "actes d'une Congrégation Romaine en particulier." In a footnote to this statement he then explains: "Le text parle des documents de chaque Congrégation prise individuellement. Un travail plus complet serait soumis aux mêmes conditions." Thereupon he cites Blat, who writes: ". . . impetrata prius licentia . . . 'uniuscuiusque Congregationis' competentis in Decretorum materia."—*Commentarium,* III, pars 2, n. 277.

[23] *Commentarium,* III, pars 2, n. 277.

Tribunals are not mentioned in canon 1389? The Code seems desirous to take account of all existing collections, but does not specify the competent authority beyond the existing Roman Congregations. Blat's view seems tenable, inasfar as any collection relates to one of the present Roman Congregations. Beyond that, liberty seems to be favored. The present law, it appears, does not take account of any collections other than those which relate to existing Congregations.

The competency of the Roman Congregations as they exist today is well outlined in the Code of Canon Law, canons 247–257. The eleven Congregations, and their respective collections of decrees, are as follows:

(a) The *Supreme Sacred Congregation of the Holy Office* was formerly the *Sacred Congregation of the Roman and Universal Inquisition.*[24] As such it possessed the collection of Farinacius, *Decisiones criminales de iudiciis et tortura,* Vicenza, 1607,[25] and Cardinal Casanata's collection of 17th century decrees;[26] Pastor also published *Allgemeine Dekrete der römischen Inquisition aus den Jahren 1555–1597* in *Historische Jahrbuch,* XXXII (1912), 479–549. For the rest, the archives of the Holy Office are secret.

The *Congregation of the Holy Office* also controls the *Index of Forbidden Books,* formerly related to the competence of the *Congregation of the Index.* The first edition of the collection was issued in 1557; it was reissued at intervals with additions and alterations. The latest edition appeared in 1940, although reprints,

[24] This Congregation was established by Paul III (1534–1549) in his Constitution "*Licet ab initio,*" 21 iul. 1542—*BRT,* VI, 244–246, but was not made a Congregation until the reign of Sixtus V, const., "*Immensa,*" 22 ian. 1588—*BRT,* VIII, 985–986.

[25] All citations of collections are taken from Van Hove, *Commentarium Lovaniense in Codicem Iuris Canonici editum a Magistris et Doctoribus Universitatis Lovaniensis,* Vol. I, tom. 1 *Prolegomena ad Codicem Iuris Canonici* (2. ed., Mechliniae-Romae: H. Dessain, 1945) unless some other source be indicated. Cf., *Ibid.,* pp. 398–402 (hereafter cited *Prolegomena*).

[26] This collection was edited by Cadène in his "Collectio decretorum responsorumque S. Officii," in *Analecta Ecclesiastica,* Revue Romaine (1893—), II (1894), 318–321, 360–362, 407–412, 493–495; III (1895), 32–33, 79–82, 115–122, 167–169, 262–263, 297–302, 352–354, 457–465, 494–498; IV (1896), 76–83, 123–128, 179–192, 273–277, 361–366, 420–421, 462–465.

with pertinent supplements, have appeared since that time, e.g., the reprint of 1946.

(b) The *Sacred Consistorial Congregation*[27] has issued no collection of its acts.

(c) The *Sacred Congregation of the Sacraments*[28] has issued no collection of its acts.

(d) The *Sacred Congregation of the Council* was originally known as the *Sacred Congregation of Cardinals for the Interpretation of the Council of Trent.*[29] It published its official *Thesaurus Resolutionum S. C. Concilii,* 167 vols., from 1718 until 1908 (Urbino, 1739–1740; Romae, 1741–1908) in folio form. Private collections were made by Zamboni in his *Collectio declarationum Card. sac. Concilii Tridentini interpretum (1700–1800)*, Romae, 1812–1816; republished at Arras, 1861–1868.—Pallottini, *Collectio omnium conclusionum et resolutionum S. C. Concilii ab anno 1564 ad annum 1860,* 17 vols., Romae, 1868–1893.—Mühlbauer, *Thesaurus resolutionum S. C. Concilii,* 7 vols., Monachii, 1867–1887.—Gamberini, *Resolutiones selectae S. C. Concilii in causis propositis per summaria precum annis 1823–1825,* Urbeveteri, 1830–1842.—Lingen-Reuss, *Causae selectae in S. C. cardinalium Concilii Tridentini interpretum propositae per summaria precum ab anno 1823 ad annum 1869,* 4 vols. in 1, Ratisbonae, 1871.—Richter-Schulte, *Canones et Decreta Concilii Tridentini . . . accedunt S. Congr. Card. Conc. Trid. Interpretum declarationes ac resolutiones (1718–1853)*, Lipsiae, 1853.

The *Sacred Congregation of the Council* today enjoys the competence of the former *Sacred Congregation of Immunity.* There were two collections: Ricci, *Synopsis decretorum et resolutionum S. C. Immunitatis,* Praeneste, 1708.—Andrea, *Synopsis, decreta et resolutiones S. Congregationis Immunitatis super controversiis iurisdictionalibus complectens,* Taurini, 1719.

---

[27] This Congregation was founded by Sixtus V under the title "Congregatio pro erectione ecclesiarum et provisionibus consistorialibus" in his Const. "*Immensa,*" 22 ian. 1588—*BRT,* VIII, 988.

[28] This Congregation was founded by Pius X (1903–1914) in his Const. "*Sapienti consilio,*" 29 iun. 1908—*AAS,* I (1909), 10.

[29] It was founded by Pius IV (1559–1565) in his Motu proprio "*Alias non nonnullas,*" 2 aug. 1564—*BRT,* VII, 300–301.

(e) The *Sacred Congregation of Religious*[80] has issued no collection of its own, but enjoys the competence of the former *Sacred Congregation of Bishops and Regulars,* which possessed Bizzarri's *Collectanea ad usum Secretariae S. C. Episcoporum et Regularium,* Romae, 1863 et 1885. This Congregation also is the successor of the former *Congregation concerning the Status of Regulars,* which had Bizzarri's *Acta S. C. super statu Regularium ab archiepiscopo Philippensi collecta,* Romae, 1862.

(f) The *Sacred Congregation for the Propagation of the Faith*[81] has issued no collection which is strictly an authentic collection. However, it has issued the *Bullarium pontificium S. C. de Propaganda Fide,* [ed. S. Bayer], 8 vols., Romae, 1839–1858.—There are also the following collections: De Martinis, *Ius pontificium de Propaganda Fide,* 8 vols., 1888–1909.—*Collectanea constitutionum, decretorum, indultorum ac instructionum Sanctae Sedis ad usum operariorum apostolicorum Societatis Missionum ad exteros cura moderatorum seminarii Parisiensis,* Paris, 1880.—*Collectanea S. C. de Propaganda Fide seu decreta, instructiones, praescripta pro apostolicis missionibus ex tabulario eiusdem S. C. deprompta,* Romae, 1893; 2. ed., 2 vols., 1907.—*Sylloge praecipuorum documentorum recentium Summorum Pontificum et S. Congregationis de Propaganda Fide necnon aliarum SS. Congregationum Romanarum ad usum missionariorum,* Città del Vaticano, 1939.—Lemmens, *Acta S. C. de Propaganda Fide pro Terra Sancta,* 2 vols., Quaracchi, 1921–1922.

(g) The *Sacred Congregation of Rites*[82] had several private collections which were later adopted as authentic collections. Pithonius, *Constitutiones pontificiae et Romanarum Congregationum ad sacros ritus spectantes,* Venetiis, 1730.—This collection was re-edited and brought up to date by Gardellini, *Decreta Authentica Congregationis sacrorum Rituum,* 7 vols., Romae, 1807–1827; a reprinting of the whole work appeared in 1827. An eighth volume was

[80] This Congregation was inaugurated by Sixtus V in his Const. "*Immensa,*" 22 ian. 1588—*BRT,* VIII, 993–994.

[81] This Congregation was established by Gregory XIII (1572–1585), but did not function as a Congregation until so constituted by Gregory XV (1621–1623) in his Const. "*Inscrutabili,*" 22 iun. 1622—*Fontes,* n. 200.

[82] This Congregation was begun by Sixtus V in his Const. "*Immensa,*" 22 ian. 1588—*BRT,* VIII, 992.

added by de Ligne in 1849. Another edition appeared in 1856–1858 at the hands of Capalti. Three appendices incorporated the acts up to the year 1888. Finally, the whole was revised and re-edited by Mühlbauer, *Decreta authentica Congregationis sacrorum Rituum et instructio Clementina ex actis ejusdem collecta ab Aloisio Gardellini in usum cleri commodiorem ordine alphabetico concinnata,* 4 vols., Monachii, 1862–1867; 7 vols., Monachii, 1873–1889.[33] The latest authentic collection, approved by Leo XIII as having the force of law is the *Decreta Authentica Congregationis Sacrorum Rituum,* 5 vols., Romae: Ex Typographia Polyglotta S. C. de propaganda Fide, 1898–1901; Appendix I (vol. VI), Romae, 1912; Appendix II (vol. VII), Romae, 1927.

The *Sacred Congregation of Rites* does the work of the former section of the *Sacred Congregation of Indulgences and Relics* which treated of relics. The *Decreta Authentica S. C. Indulgentiarum et Reliquiarum (1668–1861)*, edited by Prinzivalli in 1862, contains extremely few decrees on relics. Hence it is considered as a collection of decrees on indulgences.

(h) The *Sacred Congregation of Ceremonies*[34] was formerly a section of the *Sacred Congregation of Rites and Ceremonies.* It possesses one private collection, that of Gattico, *Acta selecta caeremonialia Sanctae Romae Ecclesiae ex variis manuscriptis codicibus et diariis saeculorum XV, XVI, et XVII,* Romae, 1753.

(i) The *Sacred Congregation for Extraordinary Ecclesiastical Affairs*[35] has issued no collection of its acts.

---

[33] The history of this collection was gathered from Van Hove, *Prolegomena,* p. 400; as well as from Lijdsman, *Introductio in Jus Canonicum cum uberiori fontium studio* (2 vols. in 1, Hilversum in Hollandia, 1924–1929), II, 396–397 (hereafter cited as *Introductio*).

[34] The Congregation of Ceremonies is certainly mentioned by Sixtus V in his Const. "*Immensa,*" 22 ian. 1588—*BRT,* VIII, 992, though some attribute the erection of this Congregation to his predecessor, Gregory XIII. The original decree cannot be found, and the Constitution "*Immensa*" allows a reading favorable to either opinion.

[35] This Congregation had several forerunners in the various pontifical commissions for individual extraordinary proceedings. It was founded on a permanent basis by Pius VII (1800–1823) in his Litt. ap., 19 iul. 1814—in Ojetti, *De Romana Curia,* pp. 130–132.

(j) The *Sacred Congregation of Seminaries and Universities* [36] has a recent collection published by the Congregation itself, the *Enchiridion clericorum: documenta Ecclesiae sacrorum alumnis instituendis* and an *Elenchus seminariorum*, Città del Vaticano, 1938.

(k) The *Sacred Congregation for the Oriental Church* [37] has issued no collection of its acts.

Failure to obtain permission to republish one of these collections does not, for that reason alone, render the collection a prohibited one. The publication would be illicit, and such a collection would never become official. Its contents would be suspect, and any author using it would run the risk of quoting false decrees, or decrees whose text may be at variance with the authentic text. Each document would have to be verified individually.[38] The same can be said, *a fortiori*, if a collection fails to observe the conditions prescribed by the Moderators of the Congregations.

(3) THE CENSORSHIP AND THE APPROVAL

When a Congregation grants permission to republish a collection of its decrees it will prescribe the conditions to be observed. The Code does not mention what these conditions are, but Augustine stated two which are certain to obtain,—the first, that the copy agree *ad litteram* with the original, the second, that a copy of the

---

[36] This Congregation was founded in the sixteenth century, apparently by Sixtus V in his Const. "*Immensa*," 22 ian. 1588—*BRT*, VIII, 992–993. During the course of succeeding centuries it practically ceased to exist. It was re-established by Leo XII (1823–1829) in his Const. "*Quod divina sapientia*," 28 aug. 1824—*Bullarii Romani Continuatio Summorum Pontificum* (19 vols., Prati, 1756–1883), XIII, 95 (hereafter cited as *BRC*).

[37] This Congregation was a special section of the Congregation for the Propagation of the Faith since the time of Pius IX (1846–1878), established in his Const. "*Romani Pontifices*," 6 ian. 1862—*Fontes*, n. 531, but was granted the status of an independent Congregation by Benedict XV (1914–1922) in his Motu prop. "*Die providentis*," 1 maii 1917, §§ IV-V—*AAS*, IX (1917), 529–531. A recent and comprehensive study of this Congregation is the dissertation of Dziob, *The Sacred Congregation for the Oriental Church*, The Catholic University of America Canon Law Studies, No. 214 (Washington, D. C.: The Catholic University of America Press, 1945).

[38] Vermeersch, *De Prohibitione*, n. 108; Pennacchi, *ASS*, XXX (1897–

reprint be sent to the Cardinal Prefect or Secretary of the respective Congregation.[39]

The Code does not even mention censorship. Yet there is no doubt that censorship must occur. It is the only adequate means to safeguard against false or adulterated decrees.[40] According to the general rule, censorship belongs to the authority from whom permission for the act of publication must be sought. Hence, the Congregation usually delegates one of its own members to perform the censorship.[41]

The censor must investigate two points of paramount importance—the genuine character of each document, and the authentic text of each document. These two facts are always certified when the Congregation grants its approval for a collection, and this document must be printed with the collection. The approval can be ordinary or extraordinary. The former merely attests to the reliability of each document and the text of each document, while the collection as such remains a private collection. The latter endows the collection with a special rank of being the authentic collection of the Congregation itself.[42]

1898), 484; De Meester, *Compendium,* III, pars 1, n. 1346; Blat, *Commentarium,* III, pars 2, n. 277; Schneider, *Büchergesetze,* p. 122; Boudinhon, *Nouv. Législ.,* p. 240; Wernz, *Ius Decretalium,* III, pars 1, n. 121, note (100); Gagnon, *La Censure,* n. 229.

[39] *Admin. Law,* p. 446.

[40] Desjardins, *Études,* LXXI (1897), 363–364; Piat, *NRT,* XXXII (1900), 12; Boudinhon, *CC,* XXI (1898), 135; Sabetti-Barrett, *Compendium,* p. 336.

[41] It is conceivable that a Congregation waive its right to perform the censorship and grant a conditional permission, i.e., provided that the diocesan censor render a favorable decision. However, the local Curia rarely has the trained specialists who can easily be found in a Roman Congregation. Furthermore, it may be necessary to consult the archives of the Roman Congregation at times to verify certain documents which the collector includes in his work. Hence, the Roman Congregation usually performs this task itself.

[42] The difference between the two can be seen from a comparison of the title pages of two different collections, e.g., *Iuris Pontificii de Propaganda Fide, auspice Emo ac Rmo Dño S. R. E. Cardinali Ioanne Simeoni S. C. De Propaganda Fide Praefecto, cura ac studio Raphaëlis de Martinis eiusdem Cong. Consult. et Missionis Sacerdotis,* Romae: Ex Typographia Polyglotta S. C. de Propaganda Fide, 1888—and—*Decreta Authentica Congregationis*

(4) THE TERM "RURSUS"

A special question arises from the presence of the term *rursus* in the text of the canon. In its obvious meaning *rursus* is to be understood as *again* or *anew.* In this sense the canon reads: "Collections of the decrees of the Roman Congregations may not be published again unless there be first obtained the permission, and unless there be previously observed the conditions prescribed by the Moderators, of the respective Congregations." This reading of the canon limits the application to existing collections of the decrees of these Congregations. It excludes the necessity of obtaining a special permission for publishing a new collection of the decrees. Certain canonists accept this literal meaning of the canon, e.g., Augustine,[43] Blat,[44] Coronata,[45] and Vermeersch-Creusen.[46] Their stand is strengthened by the fact that the word *rursus* was not found in the law as issued by Leo XIII, but was inserted into the text in 1917. Since the rest of the law was taken over verbatim from the pre-Code law, the word *rursus* attains special prominence in the new law. The old law applied to all collections, old and new, whereas the law of the Code, in view of the presence of the term *rursus,* seems limited to those collections which already are in existence.

Other commentators, however, hold that the new law means nothing more than the pre-Code law. They claim that if the present law applies explicitly to the re-publication of existing collections, then it applies, *a fortiori,* to the publication of new collections. The present law emphasizes the fact that all subsequent editions are included, but it does not wish to exclude first editions. This

---

Sacrorum Rituum ex actis eiusdem collecta eiusque auctoritate promulgata sub auspiciis SS. Domini Nostri Leonis Papae XIII, Romae: Ex Typographia Polyglotta S. C. De Propaganda Fide, 1898. The former is evidently a private collection, the latter a public or authentic collection. The approval of a collection as public or authentic can be done in various degrees, some of which imply a greater authority. For a more lengthy description of the various degrees cf. Lijdsman, *Introductio,* I, 91–93.

[43] *Admin. Law,* p. 446.

[44] *Commentarium,* III, pars 2, n. 277.

[45] *Institutiones,* II, n. 956, 3°.

[46] *Epitome,* II, n. 725.

view is held by Gagnon,[47] Woywod,[48] Wernz-Vidal,[49] Boudinhon,[50] and Jombart.[51]

In reviewing both opinions, the first seems preferable for the following reasons. There is no doubt that there is a change in the law. The old law was sufficiently clear. Hence, the insertion of *rursus* limits the new law to the existing collections. There seems to be a sufficient basis for the limitation in this that the reasons for the broader law are not as cogent after the Code as they were at the time of Leo XIII.[52]

The very presence of the Code eliminates much of the necessity that was felt for these collections at the turn of the century. Furthermore, current decrees are published in the official organ of the Holy See, the *Acta Apostolicae Sedis,* and today any diocesan censor would have little difficulty in verifying the existence and tenor of any recent decrees. Before 1900, however, this could be done most conveniently in Rome where the archives of the Congregations are kept. Hence, a restriction of the import of the pre-Code law does not seem unreasonable, and there seems likewise to be little justification to depart from the obvious meaning of the term *rursus.*

(5) SUMMARY

Canon 1389 demands that collections of the decrees of the Roman Congregations may not be republished unless there first be obtained the permission, and unless there previously be observed the conditions prescribed by the Moderators, of the respective Congregations. A collection is a mass of documents arranged in a definite order, usually chronological or systematic. All collections are contemplated, whether they include decrees of one or of more

---

[47] *La Censure,* n. 227.

[48] *Commentary,* II, n. 1404; *HPR,* XXVIII (1928), 966.

[49] *Ius Canonicum,* IV, pars 2, n. 711.

[50] " Ce n'est pas évidemment, qu'il ait voulu exempter de l'autorisation les premières éditions de ces recueils."—*Nouv. Législ.,* p. 240.

[51] Le mot *rursus* doit sans doute suggérer un raisonment *a fortiori:* s'il faut la permission pour une simple réédition, combien plus pour une collection nouvelle! "—*DDC,* III, col. 163.

[52] Pennacchi (*ASS,* XXX [1897–1898], 483–484) explained the various reasons why this law was made universal at the time of Leo XIII.

Roman Congregations, and even if they represent a suppressed Congregation, provided that the collection pertains to one of the presently existing Congregations. Periodicals, newspapers, textbooks, dissertations, theses, studies, etc., are not the equivalent of collections. The term Roman Congregation is to be taken strictly, and hence is not to be referred to the Roman Tribunals, the Pontifical Commissions, etc.

Each Congregation is the exclusive competent authority to grant the permission to reprint its own decrees. The Moderator of the Congregation is the Cardinal Prefect or Secretary with his respective advisers. Permission entails censorship, which is performed by the Congregation itself. Approval is ordinary or extraordinary, the former merely certifying the documents and the texts, but leaving the collection a private work, the latter raising the collection to the rank of the authentic collection of the Congregation. The term *rursus* implies a limitation in the present law as compared with the pre-Code law. It restricts the application of canon 1389 to the republication of existing collections; it does not apply to the publication of new collections.

CHAPTER IV

LITURGICAL BOOKS AND LITANIES

(Canon 1390)

> In edendis libris liturgicis eorumque partibus, itemque litaniis a Sancta Sede approbatis, debet de concordantia cum editionibus approbatis constare ex attestatione Ordinarii loci in quo imprimuntur aut publici iuris fiunt.

Canon 1390, as it stands in the Code, does not require the permission from Rome for the republication of the works mentioned therein. This canon empowers the local ordinaries to grant the permission and perform the censorship for the publication of liturgical books and litanies. However, a recent decree of the Sacred Congregation of Rites, while leaving the censorship of these books within the competence of the local ordinaries, ordains that a permission must be obtained from Rome each time a liturgical book is printed.[1] Hence, this canon rightfully belongs with the group of canons (1387–1391) which require special permission from Rome for the publication of the works mentioned therein.

The treatment of this canon will be divided as follows: A. Development of the law enacted in canon 1390; B. Commentary.

A. Development of the Law Enacted in Canon 1390

(1) The Law Concerning Liturgical Books

Liturgical books are those which contain the rites and prayers to be used in sacred functions, or which prescribe the sacred ceremonies accompanying the rites and prayers.[2] The Catholic Church

[1] S.R.C., decr. 10 aug. 1946—*AAS,* XXXVIII (1946), 371–372; *The Jurist* (Washington, D. C., 1941—), VII (1947), 233–234. This decree will be given full treatment within the commentary on the canon.

[2] S. R. C., decr. 17 maii 1911 ad I—*Decr. Auth.,* n. 4266.

recognizes nine liturgical books for the Latin Rite:[3] (1) The Roman Breviary; (2) the Roman Missal; (3) the Roman Pontifical; (4) the Roman Ritual; (5) the Roman Martyrology; (6) the Ceremonial of Bishops; (7) the Memorial of Rites; (8) the Roman Octavary; (9) the Collection of the Decrees of the Sacred Congregation of Rites.[4]

---

[3] Liturgical books for the Latin Rite alone will be discussed. Blat errs in holding that Orientals are also bound by this canon "*ex ipsa rei natura.*"—*Commentarium,* III, pars 2, n. 278. Orientals are bound by canon 1257 "*ex ipsa rei natura*" for that canon governs the constitution and organization of liturgical books, and consequently, the expression of dogma. Canon 1390, however, is purely disciplinary. Cf. Bouix, *De Iure Liturgico* (Parisiis, 1873), pp. 15–17; Hurley, *A Commentary on the Present Index Legislation* (Dublin, 1907), p. 140 (hereafter cited as *Commentary*); Jombart, *DDC,* III, col. 163; [Vermeersch], "De Codice et de editione cantus gregoriani"—*Jus Pontificium* (Romae, 1921—), XV (1935), 235; Pernicone, *The Ecclesiastical Prohibition of Books,* The Catholic University of America Canon Law Studies, No. 72 (Washington, D. C.: The Catholic University of America, 1932), p. 175 (hereafter cited as *Prohibition*); Michiels, *Normae Generales Iuris Canonici* (2 vols., Lublin: Universitas Catholica, 1929), I, 45.

Oriental liturgical books are the *Typikon, Leitourgikon, Euchologion, Apostolos, Psalterion, Hôrologion, Octoêkhos, Triôdion, Pentekostarion, Evangelion* (*Diaconikon*), *Menaia, Heirmologion, Anagnosis* (*Lectionarion* or *Biblion*), *Agiasmos, Anthologion, Hymnologium, Kalendarium, Menelogium,* and corresponding books in the various respective rites. See Salaville, *An Introduction to the Study of Eastern Liturgies* (adapted from the French by John Barton, London: Sands & Co., 1938), pp. 185–199 and Appendices I, II; Stella, *Institutiones Liturgicae* (2. ed., Romae, 1895), pp. 13–14. For an account of the most recent editions of Oriental liturgical books, as well as of the editions now pending see Korolevskij, "Liturgical Publications of the Sacred Congregation for the Eastern Church"—*The Eastern Churches Quarterly* (Ramsgate: St. Augustine's Abbey, 1936—), VI (1945–1946), 87–96, 388–399 (hereafter cited as *ECQ*).

[4] S. R. C., decr. 10 aug., 1946—*AAS,* XXXVIII (1946), 371–372. A previous decree of the Sacred Congregation of Rites (17 maii 1911—*Decr. Auth.,* n. 4266) had made individual mention of the Proper Masses and offices of individual dioceses and religious institutes, and the Clementine Instruction for the right ordering of the Forty Hours' Prayer. The former are merely parts of the Missal or Breviary, while the latter is included in the Collection of the Decrees of the Sacred Congregation of Rites. The Roman Octavary was not mentioned in the decree of 1911.

(a) *Legislation of Pius V (1566–1572)*

When the revised Roman Breviary was printed in 1568, Pope Pius V (1566–1572) made several rules which form the basic law for all subsequent legislation concerning liturgical books. The Breviary itself was printed in Rome, and the Pope forbade it to be printed or offered for sale in any other place without the permission of the Holy See. To facilitate obtaining the permission, the Holy Father appointed Apostolic Inquisitors (not to be confused with the local [diocesan] inquisitors) for each country. An excommunication (*latae sententiae*) was prescribed for all who acted contrary to this law. All changes, omissions and additions in the text were expressly prohibited.[5]

The new edition of the Missal appeared in 1570. It was subjected to the same law as was enacted for the Breviary. Two additional points were emphasized. Before giving permission to print a copy of the Missal, the Apostolic Inquisitor was to attest that the copy had been compared with and agreed perfectly with the Roman edition. The penalties for violations were increased.[6]

(b) *Legislation of Urban VIII (1623–1644)*

Pope Urban VIII (1623–1644) extended the same law and the same sanctions for the re-printing of the Pontifical when that first appeared in 1644.[7]

The remaining liturgical books were published by the Holy See without any sanctions of the same severe penalties in reference to an unauthorized printing of them. But it was always mentioned, without a single exception, that these books were to be reprinted without changes, omissions or additions.

When the Vulgate text of the Bible was made official, all liturgical books had to be revised so that the Scripture contained therein be conformable to the Vulgate edition. A revision was also made of the second nocturns of the Breviary, as well as a correction of the previous printer's errors and mistakes. Although the revision was begun by Sixtus V (1585–1590), it was not completed until the reign of Pope Clement VIII (1592–1605), who issued

[5] Pius V, const., "*Quod a nobis,*" 9 iul. 1568—*BRT,* VII, 685.

[6] Pius V, const., "*Quo primum tempore,*" 14 iul. 1570—*Fontes,* n. 153.

[7] Urbanus VIII, const. "*Quamvis alias,*" 17 iun. 1644—*Fontes,* n. 228.

the Breviary in 1602 and the Missal in 1604. The regulations were identical in both documents of promulgation. The Pope restricted the printing of the authentic edition to the Vatican Press, which was to be called the typical edition (*editio typica*).

Any printer was allowed to make copies of the typical edition on the condition that the local inquisitor (apparently the existence of the Apostolic Inquisitor was short-lived) or the local ordinary guaranteed that a perfect conformity existed between the copy and the typical edition. The copy was to be known as the *editio iuxta typicas,* or *editio iuxta typicam,* which, for lack of a better English equivalent, may be called an *identical* or *secondary edition.* It was also provided that an identical edition had to be made without any changes, omissions or additions. Penalties were enacted against the local inquisitors and local ordinaries who failed to safeguard the purity of the liturgical books.[8]

(*c*) *Legislation of Leo XIII* (*1878–1903*)

Pope Leo XIII (1878–1903) reorganized the entire matter concerning the censorship and prohibition of books. In his Constitution "*Officiorum ac munerum*" there was no mention of reserving the publication of typical edictions of liturgical books to the Holy See. He did mention that typical editions of the Breviary, Missal, Roman Ritual, Pontifical, Ceremonial of Bishops, and other liturgical books already approved by the Holy See were to be kept intact. Any change introduced into new editions would make them prohibited books.[9] It may be noted that this decree serves as one of the canons in the Code, i.e., canon 1399, 10°.

(*d*) *Legislation of Pius X* (*1903–1914*)

Pope Pius X (1903–1914), well known for his work in the reform of the liturgy, treated the question of liturgical books thoroughly in 1911. He distinguished clearly between typical editions and identical editions. The approval of the former pertained exclusively to the Holy See, while the approbation of the latter

---

[8] Clemens VIII, const. "*Cum in ecclesia,*" 10 maii 1602—*BRT,* X, 788–790; const. "*Cum sanctissimum,*" 7 iul. 1604—*Fontes,* n. 191.

[9] Leo XIII, const. "*Officiorum ac munerum,*" 25 ian. 1897, n. 18—*Fontes,* n. 632.

was left to the local ordinaries. The process of establishing the conformity between the two was described in detail. An *Imprimatur* was also necessary, over and above the attestation regarding the conformity. Finally, the list of the liturgical books having an official standing in the Church was recounted.[10]

(*e*) *Canon 1390*

The Code summarizes the section of the decree dealing with the identical editions into one short sentence, which serves as canon 1390 today:

> In edendis libris liturgicis eorumque partibus, [itemque litaniis a Sancta Sede approbatis,] debet de concordantia cum editionibus approbatis constare ex attestatione Ordinarii loci in quo imprimuntur aut publici iuris fiunt.

During recent years a great number of new feasts, offices, etc., have been added to the Missal and the Breviary. These deserve their rightful place in the typical editions; but it was too much to print an entire new typical edition for each new feast. Consequently it was permitted to add each new part in its proper place. To distinguish such an edition from a typical edition, and also from an identical edition, another designation was given it, i.e., *editio post typicam,* which can be called a *post-typical edition.* The Holy See alone is competent to approve such an edition, while the approval of an identical edition still remains within the competence of the local ordinary.[11]

(*f*) *The Decree of 1946*

On August 10, 1946, the Sacred Congregation of Rites issued a decree which limited the right of granting permission for the publication of an identical edition of liturgical books to the Holy See. The text reads:

---

[10] S. R. C., decr. gen. 17 maii 1911—*Decr. Auth.,* n. 4266; *AAS,* III (1911), 242.

[11] The Sacred Congregation of Rites approved the fourth post-typical edition of the Missal on December 15, 1931; the fourth post-typical edition of the Breviary on July 31, 1928; and the second post-typical edition of the Martyrology on November 1, 1928.

> 1—Uni dumtaxat Typographiae Vaticanae, ceteris exclusis, libros liturgicos typis excudendi ius esto.
>
> 2—Quilibet typographus, sive pontificio diplomate gaudet, sive non, toties a S. Rituum Congregatione licentiam obtinere debebit, quoties hos libros edere velit.
>
> 3—Administrationis Bonorum S. Sedis est pro publica horum librorum divulgatione singulis vicibus condiciones ferre.
>
> 4—Concordantia cum editione Vaticana ab Ordinario, iuxta can. 1390 Iuris Canonici, concedenda, ne subscribatur ab ipsis nisi post diligentem atque accuratam viri in re liturgica periti revisionem.
>
> 5—Ad huius decreti effectum, hi qui sequuntur liturgici libri accensentur: Breviarium Romanum, Missale Romanum, Rituale Romanum, Pontificale Romanum, Martyrologium Romanum, Caeremoniale Episcoporum, Memoriale Rituum, Octavarium Romanum, Collectio Decretorum S. Rituum Congregationis.

(2) THE LAW CONCERNING LITANIES

The Holy See has approved six litanies for the use of the universal Church: The Litany of All Saints, the Litany of the Holy Name of Jesus, the Litany of the Sacred Heart, the Litany of the Blessed Virgin Mary, the Litany of St. Joseph, and the Litany for the Dying.

(*a*) *The Decree of 1601*

The first appearance of legislation concerning litanies was a prohibition, in the beginning of the seventeenth century, which banned the use of all litanies save two, the Litany of All Saints and the Litany of Loreto. This ban was occasioned by the great number and variety of private litanies in circulation at the time,[12] some of which offended the tenor of liturgical requirements. For the future, it was decreed, the approbation of any litany would be reserved to the Holy See. The decree reads:

> Praecipit [Clemens VIII], et mandat, ut retentis antiquissimis, et communibus Litaniis, quae in Breviariis, Missalibus, Pontificalibus ac Ritualibus continentur,

[12] Musser has collected several hundred litanies in his *Kyrie Eleison* (Westminster: Newman Bookshop, 1946).

necnon Litaniis de B. Virgine, quae in Sacra Aede Lauretana decantari solent, quicumque alias Litanias edere, vel iam editis in Ecclesiis, sive Oratoriis, sive Processionibus, uti voluerint, eas ad Congregationem Sacrorum Rituum recognoscendas, et si opus fuerit, corrigendas mittere teneantur, neque sine licentia et approbatione praedictae Congregationis, eas in publicum edere aut publice recitare praesumant, sub poenis (ultra peccatum) arbitrio Ordinarii, et Inquisitoris severe infligendis.[13]

(*b*) *Legislation of Benedict XIV* (*1740–1758*)

This ruling received several confirmations during the succeeding centuries, notably through the decrees of 1727 and 1753. The latter reads:

§ IV. Quaedam ad Ritus Sacros spectantia quae prohibita sunt: 3. Litaniae omnes, praeter antiquissimas, et communes, quae in breviariis, missalibus, pontificalibus, ac ritualibus continentur, et praeter litanias de B. Virgine, quae in sacra aede Lauretana decantari solent.[14]

(*c*) *The Decree of 1860*

In 1860 the Holy Office mitigated the law. It permitted the local ordinaries to permit publications of the approved litanies, provided that they could attest to its conformity with the typical edition. However, the approbation of a new litany for public use was still reserved to Rome:

Litaniae omnes, praeter antiquissimas et communes, quae in Breviariis, Missalibus, Pontificalibus, et Ritualibus continentur, et praeter Litanias de B.M.V. quae in S. Aede Lauretana decantari solent, non edantur sine revisione et approbatione Ordinarii, nec publice in ecclesiis, publicis oratoriis et processionibus recitentur absque licentia et approbatione S. Rituum Congregationis.[15]

(*d*) *Legislation of Leo XIII* (*1878–1903*)

Pope Leo XIII (1878–1903) repeated the same law, but because

---

[13] S. C. S. Off., decr. 6 sept. 1601—*Fontes,* n. 715.

[14] Benedictus XIV, *Decreta de libris prohibitis nec in Indice nominatim expressis,* in *Index Leonis XIII,* p. xxxiv.

[15] S. C. S. Off., decr. 18 apr. 1860—*Fontes,* n. 958.

the Litany of the Holy Name of Jesus had been officially approved in the meantime, he inserted mention of it in its proper place in the text:

> Litaniae omnes, praeter antiquissimas et communes, quae in Breviariis, Missalibus, Pontificalibus, ac Ritualibus continentur, et praeter Litanias de Beata Virgine, quae in sacra Aede Lauretana decantari solent, et Litanias Sanctissimi Nominis Jesu iam a Sancta Sede approbatas, non endantur sine revisione et approbatione Ordinarii.[16]

(*e*) *Canon 1390*

The Code of Canon Law combines the question of liturgical books and litanies, and condenses their respective series of legislation into one sentence, which serves as canon 1390 today:

> In edendis libris liturgicis eorumque partibus, itemque litaniis a Sancta Sede approbatis, debet de concordantia cum editionibus approbatis constare ex attestatione Ordinarii loci in quo imprimuntur aut publici iuris fiunt.

B. Commentary

Canon 1390 states that when liturgical books and their parts as well as the litanies approved by the Holy See are to be re-published, their conformity with approved editions must be certified by the local ordinary of the place of printing or publication. The commentary on this canon will be divided as follows: (1) liturgical books and their parts; (2) litanies; (3) conformity; (4) censorship; (5) the local ordinary; (6) summary.

(1) Liturgical books and their parts

Liturgical books may be classified into two general groups, the first comprising books without chant and the second comprising books with chant,[17] i.e., chant books. A separate list will enu-

---

[16] Leo XIII, const. "*Officiorum ac munerum,*" 25 ian. 1897, n. 19—*Fontes,* n. 632.

[17] As a matter of fact, it is inaccurate to designate the first group as books "without chant"; some contain chant, e.g., the Prefaces in the Missal. However, this distinction serves better than any other division.

merate the books in each group, and a third list will be devoted to the most common editions of parts of liturgical books.

(a) *Liturgical Books Without Chant*[18]

1—The *Roman Breviary* received the earliest official approval when Pope Pius V (1566–1572) issued a new edition for the Catholic world in 1568.[19] The latest edition is that of 1914.[20]

2—The *Roman Missal* was also approved by Pope Pius V, two years subsequent to the approval of the Breviary.[21] The latest edition of the Missal was approved by the Sacred Organization of Rites in 1920.[22]

3—The *Roman Ritual* was published in 1614 by Pope Paul V (1605–1621).[23] The latest edition dates from the year 1925.[24]

4—The *Roman Pontifical* was edited in 1596 by Pope Clement VIII (1592-1605).[25] The most recent edition appears to be that of 1934.[26]

---

[18] It is quite unnecessary to cite the individual editions containing variations of the Latin Rite, e.g., the Benedictine (Breviary), the Carthusian, the Dominican (Missal), the Carmelite, the Cistercian (Missal and Breviary), the Ambrosian (used in Milan), the Mozarabic (Missal and Breviary proper to Braga in Portugal), and that of the Vatican Basilica itself (Psalter and Hymnary). Cf. Bouix, *De Iure Liturgico,* p. 135; Vermeersch-Creusen, *Epitome,* II, n. 575; Pernicone, *Prohibition,* p. 176; Korolevskij—*ECQ,* VI (1945–1946), 392.

Similarly, it is unnecessary to go into detail about the older Latin liturgical books of a more universal character, e.g., the *Sacramentarium* (*Liber Mysteriorum*), *Romani Ordines, Sacerdotale, Collectarium, Orationale, Capitulare, Homiliarium, Passionale, Poenitentiale, Processionale, Benedictionale, Exequiale.* See Stella, *Institutiones Liturgicae,* pp. 11–12.

[19] Pius V, const. "*Quod a nobis,*" 9 iul. 1568—*BRT,* VII, 685.

[20] S. R. C., decr. 25 mart. 1914—*AAS,* VI (1914), 192–193—approves the Pustet edition, while S.R.C., decr. 25 mart. 1914—*AAS,* VI (1914), 672–673 approves the Vatican edition.

[21] Pius V, const. "*Quo primum tempore,*" 14 iul. 1570—*Fontes,* n. 135.

[22] S. R. C., decr. 25 iul. 1920—*AAS,* XII (1920), 448–449.

[23] Paulus V, const. "*Apostolicae Sedi,*" 17 ian. 1614—*Fontes,* n. 198.

[24] S. R. C., decr. 10 iun. 1925—*AAS,* XVII (1925), 326. For the authors concerned in the dispute regarding the extent of the obligation of the Ritual, see Van Hove, *Prolegomena,* p. 406, note 3.

[25] Clemens VIII, const. "*Ex quo,*" 10 febr. 1596— *Fontes,* n. 180.

[26] Van Hove (*Prolegomena,* p. 406) cites this edition, but gives no further information. However, it is called the "*neueste editio typica*" by Dausend

5—The *Roman Martyrology* was printed twice before the 1584 edition received official approbation. The editions of 1582 and 1583 had to be suppressed because of the superabundance of the printer's errors. Pope Gregory XIII (1572–1585) gave the first approval.[27] The latest edition dates from 1913.[28]

6—The *Ceremonial of Bishops* was produced in 1600 by Pope Clement VIII (1592–1605),[29] and the latest edition is that of 1886.[30]

7—The *Memorial of Rites* dates from the time of Pope Benedict XIII (1724–1730), and the latest edition appeared in 1920.[31]

8—The *Roman Octavary* is a collection of the lessons of the second and third nocturns for Matins, approved by the Sacred Congregation of Rites for the use of the entire world, to be recited during certain octaves, particularly those of local patronal and titular feasts, to which an octave is not assigned in the Breviary. These lessons may be used without an indult.[32]

9—The *Collection of the Decrees of the Sacred Congregation of Rites,* although expressly mentioned in the decree of 1911,[33] and the decree of 1946,[34] needs no special explanation here.[35]

---

in the article "Pontificale Romanum" in *Lexikon für Theologie und Kirche* (10 vols., Freiburg im B.: B. Herder, 1930–1938), VIII, 372.

[27] Gregorius XIII, const. "*Emendato iam Kalendario,*" 14 ian. 1584—*Martyrologium Romanum* (Typis Polyglottis Vaticanis, 1930), p. vi.

[28] S. R. C., decr. 23 apr. 1913—*AAS,* V (1913), 278; *Fontes,* n. 6392.

[29] Clemens VIII, litt. ap. "*Cum novissime,*" 14 iul. 1600—*BRT,* X, 597–598; *Caeremoniale Episcoporum* (Parisiis, 1860), Introductio.

[30] S. R. C., decr. 17 aug. 1886—*Fontes,* n. 6176.

[31] S. R. C., decr. 14 ian. 1920—*AAS,* XII (1920), 448. Pope Benedict XIII had originally issued the *Memorial of Rites* for Rome, but it was extended to the universal Church by Pope Pius VII (1800–1823) in 1821—S. R. C., decr., 31 iul. 1821, ad I—*Decr. Auth.,* n. 2616. Subsequent pertinent decrees are: S. R. C., *Mechlinien.,* 16 (23) mart. 1876—*Decr. Auth.,* n. 3390; S. R. C., *Comen.,* 9 dec. 1899—*Decr. Auth.,* n. 4049; S. R. C., *Mediolanen.,* 22 aug. 1902—*Decr. Auth.,* n. 4101.

[32] S. R. C., *Lucionen.,* 29 dec. 1884 ad IV—*Decr. Auth.,* n. 3624. See also Wuest-Mullaney, *Matters Liturgical* (5. ed., New York and Cincinnati: F. Pustet, 1938), n. 2; Moretti, *Caeremoniale iuxta ritum romanum* (4 vols., Taurini-Romae: Marietti, 1936–1939), I, 4.

[33] S. R. C., decr. 17 maii 1911, ad IX—*Decr. Auth.,* n. 4266.

[34] S. R. C., decr. 10 aug. 1946—*AAS,* XXXVIII (1946), 371–372.

[35] The writer believes that the Collection of the Decrees of the Sacred

(*b*) *Gregorian Chant Books*

1—*The Kyriale* was published in its first typical edition in 1905.[36]

2—The *Graduale* appeared in 1907.[37]

3—The *Antiphonale* (also called *Antiphonarium*) contains the chant for the Office (except Matins), and also for the Mass. The first edition appeared in 1912.[38] A revised typical edition appeared October 18, 1919.[39]

4—The *Office of the Dead* was approved in 1909.[40]

5—The *Cantorinus* (*Toni Communiores*) was approved in 1911.[41]

6—The *Office of Holy Week* was approved in 1922.[42]

7—The *Office of the Nativity* was approved in 1926.[43]

(*c*) *Parts of Liturgical Books*[44]

Parts of liturgical books are excerpts taken from the liturgical books mentioned above, particularly such excerpts as are published

---

Congregation of Rites is governed by canon 1389 as well as by canon 1390. Many commentators merely include it among the liturgical books, e.g., Woywod, *HPR*, XXVIII (1928), 968; Augustine, *Admin. Law*, p. 191; Gagnon, *La Censure*, n. 232; Coronata, *Institutiones*, II, n. 956, 4o; Angelus-Nicolaus, *Manuale Juris Communis Regularium et Specialis Carmelitarum Discalceatorum* (Burgis: Typ. 'El Monte Carmelo,' 1929), n. 547 (hereafter cited as *Manuale*). Blat, however (*Commentarium*, III, pars 2, n. 278,) states that it is governed by 1389 rather than by 1390.

[36] S. R. C., decr. 14 aug. 1905—*Decr. Auth.*, n. 4168.

[37] S. R. C., decr. 7 aug. 1907—*Decr. Auth.*, n. 4203.

[38] S. R. C., decr. 8 dec. 1912—*AAS*, IV (1912), 727; *Decr. Auth.*, n. 4298.

[39] *Antiphonale Sacrosanctae Romanae Ecclesiae pro diurnis horis a Pio Papa X restitutum et editum et SS. D. N. Benedicti XV auctoritate recognitum et vulgatum* (Romae, 1919), p. v.

[40] S. R. C., decr. 12 maii 1909—*AAS*, I (1909), 469.

[41] S. R. C., decr. 3 apr. 1911—in Romita, *Ius Musicae Liturgicae* (Taurini: Marietti, 1936), p. 145.

[42] S. R. C., decr. 22 febr. 1922—in Romita, *Ius Musicae Liturgicae*, p. 145.

[43] See Romita, *Ius Musicae Liturgicae*, p. 145.

[44] The decree of May 17, 1911, ad IX (*Decr. Auth.*, n. 4266) indicates parts of the Breviary, Missal, Ritual and Pontifical, but does not indicate parts of the other liturgical books in the same list. The wording of the Code, however, evidently extends the "parts" to all the liturgical books without exception: "In edendis libris liturgicis eorumque partibus" (canon

separately and independently of the book from which they are derived.[45] Commentators fail to give a complete list of the parts of liturgical books in use. Among the examples they cite, the following are mentioned:

1—Parts of the Breviary are the *Psalter,*[46] the *Daily Hours* (*Horae Diurnae*),[47] the *Office of the Dead,*[48] the *Little Office of the Blessed Virgin,*[49] the *Lectionarium,*[50] the *Office of Holy Week,*[51] the *Office of the Nativity,*[52] the *Office of Pentecost,*[53] the

---

1390). Hence, commentators who mention that the present law includes parts of all liturgical books, e.g., Pernicone, *Prohibition,* p. 177, and De Meester, *Compendium,* III, pars 1, n. 1347, are to be followed rather than those who still repeat the more restricted view, e.g., Augustine, *Admin. Law,* p. 190. Curiously enough, all the parts of liturgical books in use today are taken from the four books mentioned in the decree of 1911, save the *Clementine Instruction* for the right ordering of the Forty Hours' Prayer, taken from the *Decreta Authentica* of the Sacred Congregation of Rites.

[45] Wernz-Vidal, *Ius Canonicum,* IV, pars 2, n. 711; Gagnon, *La Censure,* n. 232; Blat, *Commentarium,* III, pars 2, n. 278.

[46] Wernz-Vidal, *loc. cit.;* De Meester, *Compendium,* III, pars 1, n. 1347; Blat, *loc. cit.* The Psalter, perhaps, is the only part of a liturgical book to enjoy a typical edition of its own. Cf. S. R. C., decr. 15 ian. 1912—*AAS,* IV (1912), 83–84. The New Psalter appeared March 24, 1945. See Pius XII, motu prop., 24 mart. 1945—*Psalterium Breviarii Romani cum excerptis e communi Sanctorum secundum novam e textibus primigeniis interpretationem latinam Pii Papae XII auctoritate editum,* editio iuxta typicam vaticanam (Novi Eboraci: Benziger Bros., 1945), pp. iv–vi.

[47] Vermeersch-Creusen, *Epitome,* II, n. 725; De Meester, *loc. cit.;* Berutti, *Institutiones,* IV, p. 423; Jombart, *DDC,* III, col. 163.

[48] Berutti, *loc. cit.;* Beste, *Introductio,* p. 684; Ubach, *Theol. Moral.,* I, 558; Vermeersch, *De Prohibitione,* n. 88, 2.

[49] Beste, *loc. cit.;* Ubach, *loc. cit.;* Berutti, *loc. cit.*

[50] S. R. C., decr. 24 iun. 1914—*AAS,* VI (1914), 553.

[51] E.g., *Officium Maioris Hebdomadae et Octavae Paschatis iuxta rubricas Breviarii Romani reformatas editum* (11. ed., Ratisbonae: F. Pustet, 1931). Wernz-Vidal, *Ius Canonicum,* IV, pars 2, n. 711; Vermeersch-Creusen, *loc. cit.;* Regatillo, *Institutiones Iuris Canonici* (2 vols., Santander: Sal Terrae, 1941-1942), II, n. 242 (hereafter cited as *Institutiones*); Berutti, *loc. cit.;* Jombart, *DDC,* III, col. 163.

[52] E.g., *Officium Festorum Nativitatis et Epiphaniae Domini aliaque omnia Officia a Vigilia Nativitatis usque ad diem octavam Epiphaniae occurentia, ex Breviario Romano pro maiori recitantium commoditate digesta* (5. ed., Ratisbonae: F. Pustet, 1936).

[53] E.g., *Officium Festorum Pentecostes, SS. Corporis Christi ac Scr̃mi*

Proper Offices for individual dioceses and religious institutes,[54] and any new office.[55]

2—Parts of the Missal are the *Ordinary of the Mass,*[56] the *Missal of the Dead,*[57] the *Proper Masses* for individual dioceses and religious institutes,[58] and any new Mass,[59] altar cards,[60] the *Epistolarium, Evangeliarium, Sacramentarium* (*Liber Mysteriorum*), *Romani Ordines, Sacerdotale, Collectarium, Orationale, Capitulare, Homiliarium, Passionale, Poenitentiale, Processionale, Exsequiale* (*Agenda*), and *Benedictionale.*[61]

3—Parts of the Pontifical are the *Canon for Bishops,*[62] the *Formulae and Rubrics for Ordination,* and the *Formulae and Rubrics for Consecrating an Altar or a Church.*

4—Parts of the Roman Ritual are the *Sick-Call Ritual* and the *Marriage Ritual.*

Some books, e.g. ordinary prayerbooks, contain, along with other devotional material, certain parts of liturgical books of minor moment: either rites, ceremonies or prayers. These books are not considered liturgical books, and are not approved as such. They lack the necessary unity to be called liturgical books, even partial liturgical books.[63] They merely serve the faithful in a convenient

---

Cordis Iesu eorumque octavarum pro maiori recitantium commoditate e Breviario Romano excerptum (4. ed., Ratisbonae: F. Pustet, 1939).

[54] S. R. C., decr. gen., 19 oct. 1691—*Decr. Auth.,* n. 1852; decr. 17 maii 1911, ad IX—*Decr. Auth.,* n. 4266.

[55] E.g., the *Commune unius aut plurium Summorum Pontificum* (Neo-Eboraci: Benziger Bros., 1942). See Gagnon, *La Censure,* n. 232.

[56] Ubach, *Theol. Moral.,* I, 558. The publication of the *Ordinary of the Mass* in the vernacular follows the ordinary rules of censorship, S. R. C., *Neo-Eboracen.,* 4 aug. 1877—*Decr. Auth.,* n. 3427.

[57] Regatillo, *Institutiones,* II, n. 242.

[58] S. R. C., decr. gen. 19 oct. 1691—*Decr. Auth.,* n. 1852; decr., 17 maii 1911, ad IX—*Decr. Auth.,* n. 4266.

[59] E.g., the *Commune unius aut plurium Summorum Pontificum* (Neo-Eboraci: Benziger Bros., 1942).

[60] Fortescue-O'Connell, *The Ceremonies of the Roman Rite Described* (6. ed., London: Burns, Oates and Washbourne Ltd., 1937), p. 22 (hereafter cited as *Ceremonies*).

[61] Stella, *Institutiones Liturgicae,* pp. 11–12.

[62] Fortescue-O'Connell, *Ceremonies,* p. 23.

[63] Gagnon, *La Censure,* n. 232.

form. They may contain parts of the Breviary or the Missal,[64] such as a psalm or a group of psalms (e.g the seven penitential psalms), orations, epistles, gospels, etc.[65]

5—A part of the Collection of the Decrees of the Sacred Congregation of Rites which is often printed separately is the *Clementine Instruction* for the right ordering of the Forty Hours' Prayer. In virtue of the original decree, September 1, 1731,[66] this *Instruction* is obligatory only in Rome. Elsewhere it is recommended, save in those dioceses where other regulations are prescribed by the local ordinary.[67] It was revised to meet the demands of the latest liturgical requirements and norms in 1927.[68]

(2) LITANIES

The Litanies approved by the Holy See for the universal Church are six in number, the Litany of All Saints, the Litany of the Holy Name of Jesus, the Litany of the Sacred Heart, the Litany of the Blessed Virgin, the Litany of St. Joseph, and the Litany for the Dying. Each will be treated in turn.

(*a*) *Litany of All Saints*

The *Litany of All Saints* ranks as the oldest Litany in the

---

[64] Vermeersch-Creusen, *Epitome,* II, n. 726, 5; De Meester, *Compendium,* III, pars 1, n. 1347; Beste, *Introductio,* p. 684; Regatillo, *Institutiones,* II, n. 242; Pernicone, *Prohibition,* p. 178.

[65] Wernz-Vidal, *Ius Canonicum,* IV, pars. 2, n. 711.

[66] This Instruction of Pope Clement XII (1730–1740) [not Clement XI] forms a special appendix to Vol. III of the *Decr. Auth.,* pp. 376–383. Furthermore, an extensive commentary on this Instruction, written by Aloysius Gardellini (cf. *Decr. Auth.,* V, 201), is contained in Vol. IV, pp. 1–151.

[67] " Cum ex parte Magistri Ceremoniarum Congregationis S. Philippi Nerii Patavinae Civitatis, apud S.R.C. propositum fuerit dubium:

An Instructio pro Oratione quadraginta horarum Romae, iussu Clementis XI [sic!] primum edita, etiam extra Urbem servari possit et debeat?

S.R.C. respondit: Praedictam Instructionem extra Urbem non obligare; laudandos tamen qui se illi conformare student, nisi aliud ab Ordinariis locorum statutum sit "—S.R.C., *Patavina,* 12 iul. 1749—*Decr. Auth.,* p. 2403. It was recommended by the S.R.C., *Cadurcen.,* 9 maii 1857, ad IV—*Decr. Auth.,* n. 3409; *Lisbonen.,* 4 iun. 1874, ad I, II, III—*Decr. Auth.,* n. 3332; *Alatrina,* 18 mart. 1899, ad V—*Decr. Auth.,* n. 4015.

[68] S.R.C., decr., 27 apr. 1927—*AAS,* XIX (1927), 192–193.

Church. Its exact origin is unknown, but it seems to have been used in some form or other as early as the time of St. Gregory Thaumaturgus (+270).[69] This litany is the only one prescribed as a part of various liturgical functions. It has four forms, depending on the respective service in which it is used.

1—The ordinary and complete form (*Litaniae ordinariae*) is used in connection with various blessings, e.g., the blessing of baptismal water outside of Holy Saturday and the Vigil of Pentecost (the third form may also be used at the option of the priest), the blessing of the cornerstone of a new church, the blessing of a new church, the blessing of a cemetery, the reconciliation of a violated church or cemetery, the blessing of the people and the blessing of the fields when bestowed in virtue of an apostolic indult.[70] This form is also used in the ceremony for the conferral of Major Orders, at the consecration of a bishop, at the blessing of an abbot or of an abbess, at the blessing or consecration of virgins, at the blessing or coronation of a king, of a queen, of a queen ruler, of a king consort, at the consecration of a church, of an altar, or of a cemetery, and the opening of a synod. Furthermore, this form is used on the Rogation days, during the procession on April 25, and during other processions held, e.g., for the imploring of rain, for the repelling of tempests, for the obtaining of good weather, or those held in times of want and famine, in time of plague, in time of war, during any great tribulation, and in a procession in which the relics of saints are transferred.[71] This complete form is found in the Ritual, the Breviary, and the Pontifical.

2—The second form is used at the Forty Hours' Devotion. It is quite the same as the ordinary form, save that some invocations

---

[69] For further details and bibliography confer Francis Mershman, "Litany of the Saints"—*The Catholic Encyclopedia* (15 vols. Index, and Supplements, New York, 1907–1922), IX, 291–292.

[70] *Rituale Romanum Pauli V Pontificis Maximi iussu editum aliorumque Pontificum cura recognitum atque auctoritate Sanctissimi D.N. Pii Papae XI ad normam Codicis Iuris Canonici accomodatum* (6. ed. post typicam, Turonibus, 1936), Tit. II, c. 8; tit. VIII, c. 26–31 (hereafter cited as *Rit. Rom.*)

[71] *Rit. Rom.*, Tit. IX, c. 4, 6–12, 14.

are arranged in a different order, and a special invocation is added.[72]

3—The third form is used during the functions on Holy Saturday and the Vigil of Pentecost. It is somewhat shorter than the ordinary form. It is found in the Missal, the Gradual, and the Breviary for Holy Week. It is forbidden to use this short form on any other occasion,[73] except when the priest chooses to use this form instead of the complete form in the blessing of baptismal water outside of these two days.[74]

4—A very brief form of this litany is used in the *Ordo Commendationis Animae.*[75]

(*b*) *Litany of the Holy Name*

The *Litany of the Holy Name of Jesus* probably owes its origin to Saints Bernardine of Siena (1380–1444) and John of Capistrano (1386–1456). It was given first recognition when Pope Sixtus V (1585–1590) granted an indulgence of 300 days for its recitation. Requests for its formal approbation were consistently refused by the Holy See until Pope Leo XIII in 1886 approved it for the entire Catholic world.[76]

(*c*) *Litany of the Sacred Heart*

The *Litany of the Sacred Heart* was approved in 1898 for public recitation by the faithful.[77]

(*d*) *Litany of the Blessed Virgin*

The *Litany of the Blessed Virgin* is the second oldest of the litanies now used in the Church. Although some attempt to trace this litany as far back as the thirteenth century, it seems fairly

[72] *Rit Rom.,* Appendix. S. R. C., decr. gen. 3 apr. 1821 ad VII—*Decr. Auth.,* n. 2613.

[73] S. R. C., *Brixien.,* 17 aug. 1833— *Decr. Auth.,* n. 2709.

[74] *Rit. Rom.,* Tit. II, c. 8, n. 1–2.

[75] *Rit. Rom.,* Tit. V, c. 7, n. 3.

[76] S. R. C., *Urbis et Orbis,* 16 ian. 1886—*ASS,* XVIII (1885–1886), 509–511; *Rit. Rom.,* Tit. X, c. 1.

[77] S. R. C., *Massilien.,* 27 iun. 1898—*ASS,* XXXI (1898–1899), 190–192; S. R. C., *Urbis et Orbis,* 2 apr. 1899—*Decr. Auth.,* n. 4017; *Rit. Rom.,* Tit. X, c. 2.

well established that it was composed only toward the beginning of the sixteenth century.[78] This litany received approbation, at least by tacit consent, in 1601.[79]

(*e*) *Litany of St. Joseph*

The *Litany of St. Joseph* was approved in 1909 for public recitation.[80]

(*f*) *Litany for the Dying*

The *Litany for the Dying* is the most abbreviated form of the Litany of All Saints, to which other appropriate invocations have been added.[81]

It is customary to publish litanies in prayerbooks without seeking the attestation of the local ordinary concerning the conformity of these editions with approved editions. Ordinary censorship is deemed sufficient.[82] Certainly, these litanies are so well known that any departure from the approved forms would easily be recognized, even by the laity. Furthermore, canon 1390 is silent about translations, and outside of the liturgical books, most of the litanies appear in the vernacular.

(3) CONFORMITY

An analysis of canon 1390 shows that the canon refers to the re-editing of liturgical books and litanies already in existence. It does not govern the publication of the primary edition to which a secondary edition must conform. A commentary on canon 1390, then, must confine itself to the norms governing the re-publication

---

[78] For further historical details see Santi, "Litany of Loreto"—*The Catholic Encyclopedia*, IX, 287–290.

[79] S. C. S. off., decr. 6 sept. 1601—*Fontes*, n. 715; *Rit. Rom.*, Tit. X, c. 3.

[80] S. R. C., *Urbis et Orbis*, 18 mart. 1909—*AAS*, I (1909), 290; *Rit. Rom.*, Tit. X, c. 4.

[81] *Rit. Rom.*, Tit. V, c. 7. This litany is frequently forgotten in the listing of the litanies approved by the Church, probably because it is rarely used in public ecclesiastical functions. However, it is included by Woywod, *HPR*, XXVIII (1928), 968; De Meester, *Compendium*, III, pars 1, n. 1347; Gagnon, *La Censure*, n. 234; Augustine, *Admin. Law*, p. 200; Angelus-Nicolaus, *Manuale*, n. 548; Vermeersch, *De Prohibitione*, n. 90.

[82] Wernz-Vidal, *Ius Canonicum*, IV, pars 2, n. 711.

of liturgical books and litanies. However, before it is possible to discuss a secondary edition, and to speak of a conformity of a secondary to a primary edition, it is quite necessary to have a clear picture of the norms governing the primary edition. This will aid in clarifying the ground for the norms governing the secondary edition, and, by way of contrast, will render it easier to present, to demarcate, and to understand the points at issue.

Canon 1257 states the basic principle that the organization and approbation of liturgical books belongs exclusively to the Holy See: " Unius Apostolicae Sedis est tum sacram liturgiam ordinare, tum liturgicos approbare libros." Specific rules concerning the publication of these books are found in decrees issued by the Sacred Congregation of Rites,[83] particularly in the decree of May 17, 1911,[84] and in the decree of August 10, 1946.[85]

(*a*) *Typical or Primary Editions*

1—Editions of books concerning the Sacred Liturgy, whether they contain rites and prayers to be performed in sacred functions, or prescribe sacred ceremonies to accompany the aforesaid rites and prayers . . . are either typical (*editio typica*) or identical (*editio iuxta typicas*) editions.[86]

---

[83] The Sacred Congregation of Rites enjoys competence over liturgical matters, in virtue of canons 253 and 7.

[84] S. R. C., decr. 17 maii 1911—*Decr. Auth.*, n. 4266; *AAS*, III (1911), 242–243; *Fontes*, n. 6384.

[85] S. R. C., decr. 10 aug. 1946—*AAS*, XXXVIII (1946), 371–372; The *Jurist*, VII (1947), 233–234.

[86] Ad I—*Decr. Auth.*, n. 4266. The primary, i.e., the typical editions, are governed by canon 1257, while the secondary, i.e., the identical editions, are governed by canon 1390. There is considerable hesitancy among commentators in adopting vernacular equivalents for the Latin terms; and with good reason. The *editio typica* is easily rendered by *typical edition*, but there is no parallel for *editio iuxta typicas*. The only satisfactory equivalent seems to be the term *identical*. Woywod (*loc. cit.*) uses the technical term *reprint*, which is undoubtedly accurate, but which renders the construction of the translation very unwieldy. Blat (*Commentarium*, III, pars 2, n. 278) calls the *editio iuxta typicas* an *editio quasi-typica*, a term which gains nothing in clarity. Vermeersch (*De Prohibitione*, n. 88) calls the *editio typica* an *authentic* edition. His explanation is satisfactory, but in comparison to the *editio iuxta typicas* his term leaves much to be desired. Practically all other commentators simply retain the terms in their original form.

2—Typical editions may be published only by the Pontifical Vatican Press.[87]

3—Each single folio of the typical edition must be submitted to the censorship [revisioni] of the Sacred Congregation of Rites, which will solicit the opinion of the Liturgical Commission, or the Commission for Sacred Music and Chant, whenever feasible.[88]

4—Every typical edition shall print the decree of approval which declares such an edition to be a typical one, and which commands all publishers that future editions must absolutely conform to the aforesaid typical edition.[89]

5—The publisher must, on the completion of a typical edition, deliver two copies to the Sacred Congregation of Rites; these copies are to be preserved in the archives of the aforesaid Congregation with the utmost care and diligence.[90]

(*b*) *Identical or Secondary Editions*

1—A printer, whether pontifical or not, may not print an identical edition of a liturgical book without first obtaining the permission of the Sacred Congregation of Rites.[91]

2—This permission must be obtained anew for each subsequent edition.[92]

3—Conditions for the publication of the edition will be made in each instance by the Administration of the goods of the Holy See.[93]

4—The local ordinary shall submit the new edition to a censor skilled in liturgical matters who shall examine diligently whether

---

[87] "Uni dumtaxat Typographiae Vaticanae, ceteris exclusis, libros liturgicos typis excudendi ius esto"—S. R. C., decr. 10 aug. 1946, ad I—*AAS*, XXXVIII (1946), 371–372. The text does not mention the word *typical*, but this interpretation is necessitated by the subsequent numbers, which allow for editions by other printers, even by those who do not enjoy the rank of pontifical printers.

[88] S. R. C., decr. 17 maii 1911, ad III—*AAS*, III (1911), 242.

[89] *Ibid.*, ad I.

[90] *Ibid.*, ad V.

[91] S. R. C., decr. 10 aug. 1946 ad II—*AAS*, XXXVIII (1946), 371–372.

[92] *Ibid.*, ad II.

[93] *Ibid.*, ad III.

the new edition be in exact conformity with the typical (Vatican) edition.[94]

5—The local ordinary shall attest to the conformity of the identical with the typical (Vatican) edition.[95]

6—In regard to the publication of individual Masses and Offices proper to a diocese, and of which there is no typical edition, the local ordinary may, if a "Proper" is to be printed in the diocese where it is proper, declare, after the censorship has been duly performed, that it agrees with the original, and attach his *Imprimatur.* When there is question of printing the "Proper" of another diocese, or of some religious institute, the local ordinary within whose jurisdiction the printer resides may give his *Imprimatur* after the ordinary of the diocese or religious superior to whom the "Proper" pertains has issued a statement that the edition agrees with the original approved by the Sacred Congregation of Rites and that statement shall be printed in the edition.[96]

7—The first edition of a "Proper" which contains gregorian chant must be a typical edition.[97]

8—The re-publication of Gregorian chant books is subject to the same rules that govern the publication of other liturgical books.[98]

---

[94] This regulation is contained implicitly in canon 1393, § 3, but explicitly in the decree of 1946: "Concordantia cum editione Vaticana ad Ordinario, iuxta can. 1390 Cod. Iuris Canonici, concedenda, ne subscribatur ab ipsis nisi post diligentem ac accuratam viri in re liturgica periti revisionem."—*Ibid.*, ad IV.

[95] *Ibid.*, ad IV. This is more stringent than the wording of canon 1390, which permitted that the collation be made with any *approved* edition.

[96] S. R. C., decr. 17 maii 1911, ad VIII—*AAS*, III (1911), 242.

[97] S. R. C., *Ratisbonen.*, 24 febr. 1911, ad I—*Decr. Auth.*, n. 4260.

[98] Canon 1390 speaks of liturgical books in general. It makes no distinction between Gregorian chant books and books without chant. Hence, Coronata (*Institutiones,* II, n. 956, p. 323, n. 8 and p. 325, n. 3), Geerdinck (quoted by V[ermeersch], *Ius Pontificium,* XV (1935), 235) and Gagnon (*La Censure,* n. 233) hold that the more stringent norms which governed the republication of liturgical chant books before the Code were abrogated by canon 1390. Arguing from this principle, these authors would logically hold that the decree of 1946, which alters canon 1390, governs the republication of Gregorian chant books as well as the other liturgical books.

Augustine (*Admin. Law,* pp. 210–211), Blat (*Commentarium,* III, pars 2, n. 278) and Woywod (*Commentary,* II, n. 1405) state that the original

(4) CENSORSHIP

The censorship demanded in canon 1390, though akin to the censorship performed with a view to granting of a *nihil obstat,* does not consider the doctrinal integrity of the work. Rather, the purpose of this type of censorship is to discover and to declare the perfect conformity of the new edition with the typical (Vatican) edition. And since the Vatican edition has received the *nihil obstat* from Rome, the declaration of the conformity of the new edition with the Vatican edition is an automatic guarantee of the doctrinal integrity of the new edition.[99]

When a censor examines a liturgical book he is obliged to collate it with the most recent typical (Vatican) edition.[100] There

---

norms retain their force after the publication of the Code, but give no reason. Wernz-Vidal (*Ius Canonicum,* IV, pars 2, n. 711, (24)), however, cites decrees nn. 4166, 4178, 4260, 4263 as remaining in force in virtue of canon 2: "Quare omnes liturgicae leges vim suam retinent, nisi earum aliqua in Codice expresse corrigatur." Canon 2, it must be remembered, applies only to liturgical laws in the strict sense, i.e., those which govern rites, prayers or ceremonies. The norms governing the *printing* of liturgical books are not such. However, the strongest argument in favor of the continuance of these norms after the Code is the fact that the decree of 1946 repeats these norms;—not only for liturgical chant books, but for all liturgical books. Cf. Pius X, motu propr. "*Nostro motu proprio,*" 25 apr. 1904, ad d)—*Decr. Auth.,* n. 4134; *ASS,* XXXVIII (1905), 114; S. R. C., decr., 11 aug. 1905, ad I—*Decr. Auth.,* n. 4166; *ASS,* XXXVIII (1905), 240; S. R. C., decr. 14 aug. 1905—*Decr. Auth.,* n. 4168. It also adds new norms, as already outlined above.

[99] The need and value of such censorship is well discussed by Pernicone, *Prohibition,* p. 175, and Woywod, *Commentary,* II, n. 1405.

[100] S. R. C., decr. 10 aug. 1946—*AAS,* XXXVIII (1946), 371-372. This is a change from the previous norm, which allowed the collation to be made with any current approved edition, whether typical or identical. Cf. Blat, *Commentarium,* III, pars 2, n. 278; Gagnon, *La Censure,* n. 296; Claeys Bouuaert-Simenon, *Manuale,* III, n. 185; Arregui, *Summarium Theologiae Moralis* (13. ed., 1937, reprint by Newman Bookshop, Westminster, 1944), p. 277. However, Sipos (*Enchiridion,* p. 713, n. 18) and Noldin-Schmitt (*Summa,* II, n. 700) were still demanding that any new edition conform to a typical edition, exclusive of the identical editions.

It is forbidden to approve or publish an edition which conforms to an older edition on the plea that it represents a more critical text. Cf. S. R. C., *Societatis Presbyterorum SS. Sacramenti,* 11 mart. 1871—*Decr. Auth.,* n. 3241.

may be no additions, interpolations, omissions or mutilations.[101] The conformity between the two editions must appear even in the smallest details, e.g., regarding punctuation, position of the words, sequence of parts, grammatical rules, etc.[102] Minor printing mistakes and typographical errors, such as appear even after the most meticulous proofreading, are disregarded.[103] They do not alter the sense or order determined by the Holy See,[104] and do not constitute a formal change.[105]

The censor should be aware that no authority inferior to the Holy See, whether public or private, whether lay or ecclesiastical, is allowed to make any change in a liturgical book. This applies equally well to editors, bishops, particular councils,[106] collegiate or patriarchal churches,[107] and to any other possible source.[108] However, it is permissible to introduce certain modifications, e.g., the repetition of orations, antiphons, etc., in full as often as they occur in the Breviary or Missal for the convenience of the user.[109] The same can be said for the omission of orations, etc., which omissions would be indicated by references to the proper places where such prayers could be found.[110]

Unwarranted changes in a liturgical book, even unintentional, cause such a book to be classed as prohibited, provided that the changes are of any moment. Canon 1399, 10°, states: " [Ipso iure prohibentur] editiones librorum liturgicorum a Sede Apostolica approbatorum, in quibus quidpiam immutatum fuerit, ita ut cum

---

[101] The classic phrase "*nihil prorsus addito, dempto vel mutato*" has been repeated in almost every liturgical document concerning the publication of liturgical books since its appearance in 1568. See Pius V, const. "*Quod a nobis,*" 9 iul. 1568—*BRT*, VII, 685.

[102] S. R. C., *Societatis Presbyterorum SS. Sacramenti,* 11 mart. 1871, ad II—*Decr. Auth.,* n. 3241.

[103] Gagnon, *La Censure,* n. 296; Boudinhon, *Nouv. Législ.,* pp. 175–176.

[104] Pernicone, *Prohibition,* p. 178.

[105] Blat, *Commentarium,* III, pars 2, n. 278.

[106] Schneider, *Büchergesetze,* p. 89.

[107] S.R.C., *Urbis,* 12 maii 1612—*Decr. Auth.,* n. 297.

[108] The footnotes to canons 1257 and 1390 in the Code reveal the consistent, and even adamant, policy of the Holy See in this regard.

[109] Regatillo, *Institutiones,* II, n. 242; Pernicone, *Prohibition,* p. 178; Boudinhon, *Nouv. Législ.,* p. 175.

[110] Pernicone, *Prohibition,* p. 178.

authenticis editionibus a Sancta Sede approbatis non congruant." [111]

A liturgical book published without the attestation of the local ordinary, or of the Holy See, is not for that reason alone a prohibited book.[112] The canon mentions only one reason for the prohibition, namely, a change in the text itself. If a liturgical book contains the attestation of a local ordinary it enjoys a presumption of being in conformity with a typical edition until the contrary is proved.[113]

(5) THE LOCAL ORDINARY

The decree of 1946 states that liturgical books may not be republished until they have been collated with a typical edition, and declared conformable by an attestation of the local ordinary. Canon 1390 allows a choice between the local ordinary of the place of printing and the local ordinary of the place of publication. The law is silent about the local ordinary of the author, evidently because the text of liturgical books is already constituted, so that the persons who republish them are not authors but editors. Some commentators claim that the canon must be interpreted strictly, so as to exclude the local ordinary of the editor.[114] By far the majority allows the broader view, namely, that the attestation may be given by the local ordinary of the editor, over and above the liberty of choosing either of the two mentioned explicitly in the canon. Vidal stated that this view is supported by weighty authors (*grave auctores*), but he did not mention them by name.[115] Vermeersch-Creusen take no stand of their own, though they cite the liberal

---

[111] Pernicone, *Prohibition*, pp. 177–178.

[112] Piat, *NRT*, XXXI (1899), 134; *Theol. Mechlin.*, p. 215; Marc-Gesterman-Raus, *Institutiones*, II, 856; Laurentius, *Institutiones*, n. 633, n. 1; De Meester, *Compendium*, III, pars 1, n. 1347; Pericone, *Prohibition*, p. 178.

[113] Pernicone, *Prohibition*, p. 178.

[114] Beste (*Introductio*, p. 684) and Woywod (*HPR*, XXVIII (1928), 968) seemingly accept the strict view. Jombart (*DDC*, III, col. 164) writes: "On ne voit pas de quel droit deux ou trois commentateurs lui adjoignent le propre Ordinaire de l'auteur ou de l'editeur."

[115] *Ius Canonicum*, IV, pars 2, n. 712.

opinion of Prümmer (1866–1931) and Ferreres (1861–1936).[116] Coronata states that authors teach that the permission (i.e., attestation) of the local ordinary of the " proper author " or " proper editor " is sufficient.[117] Since the Code has remained silent, it does not seem to have excluded the third possibility. Neither does it favor it. However, the authors who support the liberal view make it probable by reason of their extrinsic authority.

(6) SUMMARY

Canon 1390 states that liturgical books and their parts as well as litanies approved by the Holy See may not be republished before the local ordinary of the place of printing or of publication attests to the conformity of the new edition with an approved edition. The decree of 1946 requires that in each instance the permission to republish a liturgical book must be obtained from the Sacred Congregation of Rites, and that the new edition must conform to a typical (Vatican) edition.

Liturgical books that have been approved by the Holy See are the *Breviary,* the *Missal,* the *Ritual,* the *Pontifical,* the *Ceremonial of Bishops,* the *Martyrology,* the *Memorial of Rites,* the *Octavary,* and the *Collection of the Decrees of the Sacred Congregation of Rites.* Approved Gregorian chant books are the *Kyriale,* the *Graduale,* the *Antiphonale,* the *Cantorinus,* the *Office of the Dead,* the *Office of Holy Week,* and the *Office of the Nativity.* Approved parts of liturgical books are the *Psalter,* the *Daily Hours,* the *Office of the Dead,* the *Office of Holy Week,* the *Office of the Nativity,* the *Office of Pentecost,* the *Little Office of the Blessed Virgin,* the *Lectionarium,* the *Evangeliarium,* any *new Office,* the *Ordinary of the Mass,* the *Missal of the Dead,* any *new Mass, altar cards,* the *Canon for Bishops,* the *Proper Masses and Offices* of dioceses or religious institutes, the *Clementine Instruction* for the right ordering of the Forty Hours' Prayer, the *Sick-Call Ritual,* the *Marriage Ritual,* and possibly others. The approved litanies are the *Litany of All Saints,* the *Litany of the Holy Name,* the

---

[116] *Epitome,* II, n. 726, 5°; Prümmer, *Manuale,* q. 416; Ferreres, *Institutiones,* II, n. 385.

[117] *Institutiones,* II, n. 956, 4°.

Litany of the Sacred Heart, the *Litany of the Blessed Virgin,* the *Litany of St. Joseph* and the *Litany for the Dying.*

Typical (primary) editions of liturgical books are reserved exclusively to the Holy See by canon 1257, and also by the decree of 1946. Secondary (identical) editions are governed by canon 1390 and by the decree of 1946. Hence, secondary editions may not be published by any printer without the permission of the Sacred Congregation of Rites, and without an attestion of conformity to the typical edition; which attestation is to be issued by the local ordinary only after the censorship has been performed by a qualified liturgical expert.

Identical editions must conform to typical editions. The typical edition used as the basis for comparison must be the most recent edition. Censorship consists in collating the two editions and verifying the absolute conformity of the new edition with the typical edition. If the approval (not to be identified with the permission) for the new edition has been given by the Holy See, any changes (additions, omissions or alterations) in that edition, whether intentional or not, render such an edition prohibited. Minor printing mistakes, such as escape even the most meticulous proofreaders, are disregarded. A lack of attestation of conformity in an edition does not, for that reason alone, render the edition prohibited; but it does render it suspect.

The Code demands that the attestation of conformity be given by the local ordinary of the place of printing or of publication. However, there is sufficient extrinsic authority to allow the attestation to be made by the local ordinary of the editor (there is no real author). Any of the three local ordinaries mentioned in canon 1385, § 2, may give the attestation and the *Imprimatur.*

CHAPTER V

TRANSLATIONS OF THE SACRED SCRIPTURES

(Canon 1391)

> Versiones sacrarum Scripturarum in linguam vernaculam typis imprimi nequeunt, nisi sint a Sede Apostolica probatae, aut nisi edantur sub vigilantia Episcoporum et cum adnotationibus praecipue excerptis ex sanctis Ecclesiae Patribus atque ex doctis catholicisque scriptoribus. (Canon 1391)

A. Development of the Law Enacted in Canon 1391

There was a real need, in the early Church, to safeguard the pure transmission of the entire body of the Sacred Scriptures. Defective translations were a menace to the faithful, and hence they were banned. Apocryphal versions were proscribed at an early date. A great impetus was given to this disciplinary precaution after the Canon of Sacred Scripture had been definitely established.[1] Thus the early Church controlled the malice of heretics and the mistakes of *bona fide* Catholics until the invention of printing.[2] It was a problem of the prohibition of books rather than that of censorship.

(1) Legislation of Innocent III (1198–1216)

The attitude of the Holy See toward translations of the Bible is outlined in a response given by Pope Innocent III in 1199 to the Bishop of Metz. The latter inquired about the method of procedure against certain groups in his diocese who were abusing translation of the Sacred Scriptures. The response is given partially in the following text:

---

[1] *De Libris Recipiendis et Non Recipiendis,* better known as the *Decretum Gelasianum—BRT,* I, 122–126.

[2] Pernicone, *Prohibition,* p. 26–64.

> . . . Licet autem desiderium intelligendi divinas scripturas, et secundum eas studium adhortandi, reprehendendum non sit, sed potius commendandum; in eo tamen apparent quidem laici . . . officium praedicationis Christi sibi usurpant, sacerdotum simplicitatem eludunt, et eorum consortium aspernantur, qui talibus non inhaerent. . . .[3]

From this it is evident that originally there was no prohibition of translating the Bible, and that Pope Innocent himself made none. However, such a prohibition did come into being shortly after the time of Innocent III. Various provincial councils enacted legislation against the possession and the reading of certain translations of the Bible on the grounds that these translations were dangerous. A person who kept them made himself suspect of heresy.[4]

In the beginning of the fifteenth century one sees a development of the idea of censorship relative to translations of the Bible before their publication was allowed. The provincial council of Oxford (1408) enacted the following:

> Statuimus igitur et ordinamus ut nemo deinceps aliquem textum sacrae Scripturae, auctoritate sua, in linguam Anglicam vel in aliam transferat . . . nec legatur aliquis huiusmodi liber . . . quousque per loci dioecesanum, seu, si res exigeret, per concilium provinciale, ipsa translatio fuerit approbata.[5]

(2) LEGISLATION OF THE V GENERAL COUNCIL OF THE LATERAN (1512–1517)

The requirement of the previous censorship of books did not become a universal law in the Church until the end of the fifteenth and the beginning of the sixteenth century. Pope Leo X (1513–1521) made the following law:

> Statuimus et ordinamus, quod de cetero perpetuis fu-

[3] C. 12, X, *de haereticis*, V, 7.

[4] E.g., Council of Toulouse (1229), canon 14—Mansi, XXIII, 197; Council of Tarragona (1223), canon 2—Mansi, XXIII, 329.

[5] Council of Oxford (1408), canon 7—Mansi, XXVI, 1038. It may be of interest to observe that this very same Council, although so lenient in its legislation, prohibited the translation made by Wyclif (1320–1384).

> turis temporibus nullus librum aliquem seu aliam quamcumque scripturam . . . imprimere seu imprimi facere praesumat, nisi prius . . . diligenter examinentur. Qui autem secus praesumpserit, ultra librorum impressorum amissionem, et illorum publicam combustionem, ac centum ducatorum fabricae Principis Apostolorum de Urbe sine spe remissionis solutionem, ac anni continui exercitii impressionis suspensionem, excommunicationis sententia innodatus existat. . . .[6]

This legislation was very general in character. In the course of time it received further explanations. The Council of Trent specified several things which were fully included in this law, among them being the mention of scriptural works. It referred explicitly to the translations of the Bible, but only inasfar as such translations were or were not allowed to the faithful for general reading. It left the approbation of translations in the hands of the bishops, who had always been competent in this matter.[7]

(3) LEGISLATION OF BENEDICT XIV (1740–1758)

The next advance in general legislation came at the bidding of Pope Benedict XIV, who issued the following regulation through the Sacred Congregation of Rites:

> Quod si huiusmodi versiones vulgari linga fuerint ab Apostolica Sede approbatae, aut editae cum adnotationibus desumptis ex sanctis Ecclesiae patribus, vel ex doctis, catholicisque viris, conceduntur.[8]

This new law made explicit the fact that the Holy See could

[6] Leo X (in Conc. Lateranens. V), const. "*Inter sollicitudines,*" 4 maii 1515, §§ 2-3.—*Fontes,* n. 68.

[7] Conc. Trident., sess. IV, *de canonicis scripturis.* It is proper to note that the *De libris prohibitis* . *Regulae Decem,* nn. 3-4 refer primarily to the *reading* of translations of the Sacred Scriptures, and only by way of inference to the printing or publication of such versions in the vernacular. It was under Pope Leo XIII (1878-1903) that the two notions were separated and given appropriate attention. Cf. Gagnon, "La Lecture des Livres par les fidèles"—*Semaine Religieuse de Quebec* (Quebec, 1899—), LV (1944), 246-253.

[8] S. R. C., decr. 13 iun. 1757—*Fontes,* n. 5145.

approve any translation of the Sacred Scripture, whether it contained the designated notes or whether it was printed without them. The local ordinary, on the other hand, was to approve only those translations which were edited with notes taken from the Fathers of the Church or from other learned, Catholic scholars. Unfortunately, the compliance with this regulation was unsatisfactory. Some translators palmed off distorted interpretations and bolstered their views with texts from the Fathers cited erroneously, and understood still more erroneously.[9] Hence, this decree was repeated time and time again during the next century and a half,[10] and was finally improved under Pope Leo XIII.

(4) LEGISLATION OF LEO XIII (1878–1903)

Pope Leo XIII finally made the reading and the printing of vernacular translations of the Scriptures a matter of separate though parallel legislation. Still, the break was not complete. The text is:

> Cum experimento manifestum sit, si Sacra Biblia vulgari lingua passim sine discrimine permittantur, plus inde, ob hominum temeritatem detrimenti, quam utilitatis oriri; versiones omnes in lingua vernacula etiam a viris catholicis confectae, omnino prohibentur, nisi fuerint ab Apostolica Sede approbatae, aut editae sub vigilantia Episcoporum cum adnotationibus assumptis ex Sanctis Ecclesiae Patribus, atque ex doctis catholicisque scriptoribus.[11]

---

[9] Zaccaria (1714–1795), writing twenty years after the appearance of the decree of 1757, cited a number of French and Italian vernaculars which were condemned by the Holy See, and then continued: "Da tutto ciò io raccolgo, che senza l'approvazione della Sede Apostolica non avremo mai una Bibbia volgare di sicura fedeltà . . . Chi sá quali Interpreti si facessero da un Volgarizzatore passare per Catholici . . . che tutti gli errori si possone confermare con testi di Santi Padri mal citati, e peggio intesi "—*Storia polemica delle proibizione de' libri* (Romae, 1777), pp. 361–362 (hereafter cited as *Storia Polemica*).

[10] S. C. Indicis, decr. 23 iun. 1817, n. 6—*Fontes,* n. 502, ftn. 6; S. R. C., monitum, 7 ian. 1836—*Fontes,* n. 5148; Pius IX, ep. encycl. "*Nostis et Nobiscum,*" 8 dec. 1849, in *Pii IX Pontificis Maximi Acta* (9 vols., Romae, 1854–1878), I, 207–208; Pius IX, const. "*Apostolicae Sedis,*" 12 oct. 1869—*Fontes,* n. 552.

[11] Leo XIII, const. "*Officiorum ac munerum,*" 25 ian. 1897, n. 7—*Fontes,* n. 632.

The first section of this text, "*Cum experimento . . . oriri,*" was taken verbatim from Rule IV of the Tridentine Rules Concerning Prohibited Books. The second section was new. The third section, beginning with "*nisi fuerint . . .*" and continuing to the end, was taken almost verbatim from the decree of Pope Benedict XIV in 1757, with the exception of the phrase "*sub vigilantia Episcoporum.*" Before the time of Leo XIII it was always understood that the bishop could approve such versions; but thereafter he was instructed to exercise vigilance. This law has now become incorporated in the Code and is placed in its proper section among the canons concerning the prohibition of books, namely under canon 1399, 5°.

Pope Leo's legislation concerning censorship properly so called was as follows:

> Penes quos potestas sit sacrorum bibliorum editiones et versiones adprobare vel permittere ex iis liquet quae supra (n. 7) statuta sunt.[12]

This law made certain that the censorship and approbation of translations of the Sacred Scriptures rested in the hands of the bishops as well as of the Holy See.

(5) CANON 1391

One naturally expects a goodly portion of the previous law to be repeated in the section of the Code concerning the printing of vernacular translations of the Sacred Scriptures. The new text of canon 1391 is taken partly from n. 7 and partly from n. 30 of the Constitution "*Officiorum ac munerum.*" It reads:

> Versiones sacrarum Scripturarum in linguam vernaculam typis imprimi nequeunt, nisi sint a Sede Apostolica probatae, aut nisi edantur sub vigilantia Episcoporum et cum adnotationibus praecipue excerptis ex sanctis Ecclesiae Patribus atque ex doctis catholicisque scriptoribus.

B. COMMENTARY

Canon 1391 states that translations of the Sacred Scriptures

[12] Leo XIII, *ibid.*, n. 30—*Fontes*, n. 632.

in the vernacular may not be printed unless they have been approved by the Apostolic See, or unless they are published under the vigilance of the bishops and are provided with notes taken principally from the Holy Fathers of the Church and from learned, Catholic writers. The commentary will be divided as follows: (1) translations; (2) approval; (3) censorship; (4) notes; (5) parts of the Bible; (6) prohibition; (7) summary.

(1) TRANSLATIONS

Canon 1391 is concerned with translations of the Sacred Scriptures made by Catholics. Any Catholic, priest or religious, layman or laywoman, who possesses sufficient linguistic and theological knowledge may make a translation. Translations made by non-Catholics are not a matter for previous censorship. Rather, they are prohibited *ipso iure,* as is evident from canon 1399, 1°: " [*ipso iure prohibentur*] editiones textus originalis et antiquarum versionum sacrae Scripturae, etiam Ecclesiae Orientalis, ab acatholicis publicatae; itemque eiusdem versiones in quamvis linguam, ab eisdem confectae vel editae." [13]

The language from which the translation is made may be any of the ancient texts. It is not necessary to use the Vulgate. The language into which the Bible is translated may be any vernacular language, i.e., a living language used by a people today.[14] Such are, for example, English, French, Spanish, Italian, German, Polish, Chinese, Japanese, Russian, Indian, any modern Slav language, etc. Canon 1391 does not apply to a translation into a dead language, e.g., into Latin, or into any of the ancient languages, e.g., the old Syriac.[15]

It is quite immaterial whether the translation be of the entire Bible, or of a part of the Bible, e.g., the Thorah (Law), the Nebiyim (Prophets), the Ketubim (Didactic books), the Gospels,

[13] Hence Augustine (*Admin. Law,* p. 447) is incorrect in stating that canon 1391 applies to all translations in a vernacular language, whether the translator is a Catholic or a non-Catholic.

[14] Augustine, *loc. cit.;* Schneider, *Büchergesetze,* p. 66; Blat, *Commentarium,* III, pars 2, n. 279; Gagnon, *La Censure,* n. 236; Berutti, *Institutiones,* IV, 421; Jombart, *DDC,* III, col. 164.

[15] Augustine, *loc. cit.;* Ayrinhac, *Admin. Legisl.,* p. 284.

the Epistles, or whether the translation be of only one book of the Bible.[16] However, it is imperative to remember that canon 1391 speaks only of *translations,* and not of the many other allied works on the Bible, e. g., commentaries, concordances, diatessara, treatises, etc.[17] The writer includes in this group the "paraphrastic" versions of the Bible, i.e., those whose text is intercalated with explanatory and supplementary material.[18] Paraphrases are not pure translations and cannot be quoted as pure Scripture. Rather, they present a text considerably altered by the introduction of foreign material. These so-called versions are governed, not by canon 1391, but, like other treatises, by canon 1385, § 1, 1º.[19]

(2) APPROVAL

A vernacular version of the Bible may be approved by the Holy See or by the bishops. If the approval is sought from the Apos-

---

[16] Augustine, *loc. cit.* The translation of parts of the Bible smaller than an individual book will be treated separately.

[17] Pernicone, *Prohibition,* p. 144; Hurley, *Commentary,* p. 75.

[18] Vermeersch, *De Prohibitione,* n. 71, 5º; Cappello, *De Curia Romana,* I, 280; Gagnon, *La Censure,* n. 291; De Meester, *Compendium,* III, pars 1, n. 1348; Tummulo-Iorio, *De Censuris,* n. 1022, 5º.

[19] Pernicone, *Prohibition,* p. 144; Hurley, *Commentary,* p. 76. Most of the commentators treat paraphrastic versions as translations governed by canon 1391, and claim that they fulfill the conditions of the canon inasmuch as they contain notes virtually or equivalently, e.g., Vermeersch, *De Prohibitione,* n. 71; Arndt, *De Libris Prohibitis Commentarii* (Ratisbonae, 1895), p. 129; Piat, *NRT,* XXX (1898), 473; Van Coillie, *Commentaria in constitutionem SSmi Dni Leonis XIII* "OFFICIORUM AC MUNERUM" (Brugis, 1899), pp. 43–44 (hereafter cited as *Commentaria*); Marc-Gestermann-Raus, *Institutiones,* I, 856; Ubach, *Theol. Moral.,* I, 558; Tummulo-Iorio, *De Censuris,* n. 1022, 5º; Ayrinhac, *Admin. Legisl.,* p. 284; Ferreres, *Institutiones,* II, n. 388, 4º; Genicot-Salsmans, *Institutiones Theologiae Moralis* (14. ed., 2 vols., Buenos Aires: Dedebec, Ediciones Desclee, De Brouwer, 1939), I, n. 453; Périès, *L' Index, Commentaire de la constitution apostolique* "OFFICIORUM" (Paris, 1898), p. 83 (hereafter cited as *L'Index*); Heymans, *De ecclesiastica librorum aliorumque scriptorum in Belgia prohibitione disquisitio* (Bruxellis, 1849), n. 198; Moureau, *La Nouvelle législation de l'Index* (Lille, 1898), p. 49 (hereafter cited as *Législation*); Vermeersch-Creusen, *Epitome,* II, n. 726, 6º; De Meester, *Compendium,* III, pars 1, n. 1348; Cappello, *De Curia Romana,* I, 280; Gagnon, *La Censure,* n. 291; Jombart, *DDC,* III, col. 164; Beste, *Introductio,* p. 684.

tolic See the translation may, but need not, have notes.[20] The approval is given by the Holy Office, acting in the name of the Holy See.[21]

If the approval is sought from the bishop,[22] the translation must contain notes. This was always demanded, either explicitly or implicitly. A doubt arose, however, when the Code adopted the text of Leo XIII and inserted "*et*" between "*sub vigilantia Episcoporum*" and "*cum adnotationibus.*" Some commentators began to argue that if "*et*" be understood copulatively, then both the vigilance of the bishops and the use of the notes were required; but if "*et*" be understood disjunctively, the edition could either be edited under the vigilance of the bishops, or it could have notes. The theoretical doubt was settled by the Pontifical Commission for the Authentic Interpretation of the Code in favor of the copulative (traditional) interpretation of "*et.*"[23] Any bishop[24] mentioned in canon 1385, § 2, may give the approval,[25] but only after the censorship has been performed.

[20] It is a significant fact that the Holy See does not approve a vernacular version without notes. Cf. Augustine, *Admin. Law,* p. 448; Wernz, *Ius Decretalium,* III, pars 1, n. 111 (58); De Meester, *Compendium,* III, pars 1, n. 1348; Woywod, *HPR,* XXVIII (1928), 969; Vermeersch, *De Prohibitione,* n. 71, 3o; Pernicone, *Prohibition,* p. 143; Gagnon, *La Censure,* n. 235; Jombart, *DDC,* III, col. 164. Schneider alone (*Büchergesetze,* p. 68) stated that such an approval happens seldom; most of the others stated that it never happens.

[21] Canons 7 and 253; Blat, *Commentarium,* III, pars 2, n. 279.

[22] Canon 1391 is very explicit, and Seraphinus a Loiano has no foundation for his statement: "Requiritur quoque licentia Sedis Apostolicae ad primam editionem versionum Sacrarum Scripturarum in linguam vernaculam."—*Institutiones Theologiae Moralis ad normam Codicis Iuris Canonici,* II, 632.

[23] 20 maii, 1923—*AAS,* XVI (1924), 115.

[24] Coronata (*Institutiones,* II, 956, 5°) holds that the use of the term "*Episcopus*" instead of "*Ordinarius loci*" in canon 1391 excludes the Vicar Capitular and the Vicar General. Similarly, Salucci (*Il Diritto Penale Secondo il Codice di Diritto Canonico* [2 vols., Subiaco: Typografia dei Monasteri, 1926–1930], II, 36, n. 1, hereafter cited as *Il Diritto Penale*) maintains that "*Episcopus*" does not mean "*Ordinarius.*" It is true that the term "*Episcopus*" is used, but there does not seem to be sufficient justification to limit it in this way. The Code has not changed the law, and therefore the norm of canon 6, 2o, obtains.

[25] Blat, *Commentarium,* III, pars 2, n. 279; Pernicone, *Prohibition,* p. 143; Bouscaren-Ellis, *Canon Law,* p. 709.

(3) CENSORSHIP

The censorship of a translation pertains to the authority who grants the approval for its publication. If the Holy See is to grant the approval, it will perform the censorship. However, the Holy See approves only those translations which are of outstanding merit.[26] All others it remits to the bishops. The chief merits of a translation are its fidelity, lucidity and elegance, while the chief merits of the notes are their fidelity, clarity and brevity.[27]

The Holy See does not demand absolute fidelity to the Vulgate. On the contrary, Pope Pius XII in his recent encyclical "*Divino afflante Spiritu*" indicated the full liberty, and even the necessity, of calling any ancient text to the potential aid of the translator:

> . . . atque adeo eiusmodi [Vulgatae] *authentica* non primario nomine *critica,* sed *iuridica* potius vocatur. Quapropter haec Vulgatae in rebus doctrinae auctoritas minime vetat—immo id hodie fere postulat—quominus eadem haec doctrina ex primigeniis etiam textibus comprobetur et confirmetur, atque etiam quominus passim in auxilium iidem textus vocentur, quibus recta Sacrarum Litterarum significatio ubique magis in dies patefiat atque explanetur. Ac ne id quidem Tridentini Concilii decreto prohibetur, quominus nempe ad christifidelium usum et bonum et ad faciliorem divini eloquii intelligentiam, conversiones in vulgatas linguas conficiantur, eaeque etiam ex ipsis primigeniis textibus, ut iam multis in regionibus, approbante Ecclesiae auctoritate, laudabiliter factum esse novimus.[28]

If the bishop grants the approval, it is his duty to perform the censorship, either personally or through others. There is considerable difference of opinion concerning the exact meaning of the phrase "*sub vigilantia Episcoporum.*" This phrase first appeared in the law in 1897. Since that time it has received numerous interpretations. Pennacchi (+1898) and Schneider

---

[26] Boudinhon, *Nouv. Législ.*, p. 108.

[27] Ubaldi, *Introductio in Sacram Scripturam ad usum Scholarum Pont. Seminarii Romani et Collegii Urbani de Propaganda Fide* (4. ed., 3 vols., Romae, 1891), III, 352–372 (hereafter cited as *Introductio*).

[28] 30 sept. 1943—*AAS,* XXXV (1943), 309–310. In all doctrinal matters the authority of the Vulgate is supreme and exclusive.

(+1906) held that a bishop, either personally or through a competent censor, was to render a judgment on the fidelity of the translation and the suitability of the notes.[29] Others were less precise, stating merely that vigilance meant special care.[30]

Still others demanded a careful comparison of the translation with the original (Vulgate!) text, or at least with another translation already approved by the Holy See.[31] Claeys Bouuaert-Simenon hold that the vigilance is exercised if the bishop, in giving the *Imprimatur,* divulges the names and particular functions of the Scriptural specialists employed in the translation.[32] Gagnon, basing his view on the recent encyclical "*Divino afflante Spiritu*" of Pope Pius XII, states that vigilance consists in a scrutiny of the theological orthodoxy of the translation which is based on the work of competent critics and exegetes.[33]

The writer holds that vigilance is more than ordinary censorship, but not actual supervision. A bishop exercises vigilance by entrusting the censorship to a qualified expert in Scriptural studies, who will test the translation regarding its doctrinal and linguistic fidelity to the text from which it is taken, and also regarding the suitability of the notes. In case of a conflict between fidelity to

---

29 Pennacchi, *AAS,* XXX (1897–1898), 183; Schneider, *Büchergesetze,* p. 68.

30 E.g., *Theol. Mechlin.,* p. 205, n. 1: "Vigilantia nedum importat rei notitiam sed curam ut agenda rite peragantur, et praescriptioni legis respondeant"; Vermeersch (*De Prohibitione,* n. 71, 4°) held that a "specialis cura de istis versionibus ab episcopis habenda est," which view was repeated in Vermeersch-Creusen, *Epitome,* II, 726, 6°. Bouscaren-Ellis (*Canon Law,* p. 709) write: "The vigilance of the Bishops means special care on their part in approving the work, not actual supervision." Blat (*Commentarium,* III, pars 2, n. 279) has: "Fiant et imprimantur sub vigilantia Episcoporum."

31 Augustine (*Admin. Law,* p. 448) writes: "A difficulty may arise from the fact that, with the exception of the Latin Vulgate, there is no approved original text—the Greek text, and much more so the Hebrew Massoretic text, being subject to many variants. The episcopal censor, therefore, had better keep to the Latin text, but he may make use of the original in doubtful cases." Coronata, *Institutiones,* II, n. 956, 5°; Wernz-Vidal, *Ius Canonicum,* IV, pars 2, n. 711; Pernicone, *Prohibition,* p. 143; Jombart, *DDC,* III, col. 164.

32 *Manuale,* III, n. 185.

33 *La Censure,* n. 290.

the doctrine of the text and fidelity to the doctrine of the Vulgate, the latter must be followed.

At the II Plenary Council of Baltimore in 1866 the American Hierarchy was desirous of adopting a vernacular version for the United States. The Sacred Congregation for the Propagation of the Faith gave the following norm:

> . . . S. Congregatio voluit, . . . attento gravi Catholicorum periculo in Statibus Federatis Biblia ab haereticis corrupta prae manibus habendi, recognitionem versionis Anglicae Duacensis opportunam videri; et licet S. Sedes ab huiusmodi versionibus sua approbatione firmandis aliena sit, Te [Arch. Spalding, Apostolic Delegate to the Second Plenary Council of Baltimore] tamen rem utilem atque etiam Concilii Baltimorensis anni 1858 votis consonam facturum, si adscitis viris theologicis, rerum Biblicarum peritis, comparatis inter se nedum variis editionibus versionis Duacensis, sed etiam aliis versionibus Anglicis, si quae extent praeter Duacensem, Catholico spiritu elaboratis, reliquisque diligentiis adhibitis in suppresso [decreto] N°. 17 [Cap. III] propositis, praedictae versionis Duacensis emendationem aggrederetur. Si enim nova haec editio nil desiderandum relinqueret, sperare licet aliarum Dioecesium Episcopos illi esse paullatim suffragaturos, atque ita futurum ut, re proposita in alio Plenario Concilio, pro communi fidelium usu, ad exclusionem versionum caeterarum, approbari mereretur.[34]

It is desirable that every nation have the Sacred Scriptures in its vernacular language. Boudinhon (1858–1941) suggested that, to assure the people of a reliable version, the bishops of a country approve one version for public use in all prayerbooks, public prayers, sermons, etc., without prohibiting other versions in the same language for private use.[35] The United States possesses the recent Confraternity Edition of the New Testament, published in 1941. It contains the approval of the American Hierarchy, but is not enjoined as the official text of the country.

---

[34] Instructio, 24 ian. 1868—*Concilii Plenarii Baltimorensis II Acta et Decreta* (2. ed., Baltimorae, 1894), lxii–lxiii.

[35] *Nouv. Législ.*, p. 109.

(4) NOTES

Canon 1391 requires the presence of notes in translations, at least in those editions which are approved by the bishops. Neither the Code nor any other law of the Church determines the nature of the notes, their purpose, kind, number, author, or the passages to which they may or must be appended.

Notes are brief explanatory remarks or comments on particular words or passages in the text. Formerly they were known as *glossae* or *scholia,* while today they are generally known as annotations or notes.[36] Their content may be extremely varied, e.g., theological, moral, philological, profane (from the natural sciences), etc.

Notes serve to clarify the text and make it more easily understood. They prevent an erroneous interpretation, especially in difficult or obscure passages. They also elaborate texts which, in the opinion of the translator, require the explicit teaching of approved Catholic writers.[37] This is effected through a presentation of the traditional explanation of the text according to the mind of the Church.[38]

Notes may contain the opinions of the Fathers or of other writers in various forms. Actual opinions may be quoted verbatim, or they may be given in an edited or mediate form.[39] The mediate kind of note readily lends itself to brevity and condensation,[40] though any kind of note is admissible, provided that it be genuine.[41]

The Code is indifferent regarding the number of notes, few

[36] Ubaldi, *Introductio,* III, 370–372; Grannan, *A General Introduction to the Bible* (4 vols., St. Louis, 1921), IV, 174–176.

[37] Hurley, *Commentary,* pp. 74–75.

[38] Blat, *Commentarium,* III, pars 2, n. 279; De Meester, *Compendium,* III, pars 1, n. 1348; Claeys Bouuaert-Simenon, *Manuale,* III, n. 185; Gagnon, *La Censure,* n. 291.

[39] Boudinhon, *Nouv. Législ.,* p. 108; Ayrinhac, *Admin. Legisl.,* p. 284; Nevin, "Censorship of Books"—*Australasian Catholic Record,* Sidney, 1924—), II (1925), Claeys Bouuaert-Simenon, *Manuale,* III, n. 185; Vermeersch, *De Prohibitione,* n. 71, 5°; Cappello, *De Curia Romana,* I, 280; Wernz, *Ius Decretalium,* III, pars 1, n. 111 (58); Pernicone, *Prohibition,* p. 144; Noldin-Schmitt, *Summa,* II, n. 701.

[40] Tummulo-Iorio, *De Censuris,* n. 1022, 5°.

[41] Augustine, *Admin. Law,* p. 448; Gagnon, *La Censure,* n. 291.

or many, that appear with a translation. It is also indifferent regarding their place on the page, whether in the margin or at the foot of the page, and even regarding their place in the book itself, whether at the end of a chapter or at the end of the book.[42]

In the preface to the Clementine edition of the Vulgate there was incorporated a prohibition to add variant readings of the other manuscript bibles in the margin of the Vulgate text. The Pontifical Biblical Commission issued a declaration to the effect that at the bottom of the page such variant readings were allowed as an aid for students.[43]

The phrase, "*in editionibus versionis Vulgatae,*" employed in this decision points to editions of the Vulgate [Latin] version of the Scriptures, and not to versions [translations or vernaculars] of the Vulgate edition, as is stated by some commentators.[44] It should be clear that this prohibition, as well as the decision of the Pontifical Biblical Commission, refers only to the Vulgate, and not to vernacular versions. Hence, it really does not relate to the matter treated in canon 1391, though many commentators regard it as having application to the content of this canon.

Canon 1391 states that the notes must be taken principally from the Fathers of the Church and from learned, Catholic writers.[45] The term "principally"—*praecipue*—means that the majority of the notes are to be taken from the Fathers and learned Catholic writers,[46] while allowing that some notes be drawn from scholars who are not Catholics.[47]

---

[42] Blat, *Commentarium,* III, pars 2, n. 279; Beste, *Introductio,* p. 684.

[43] 17 nov. 1921—*AAS,* XIV (1922), 27.

[44] Ubach, *Theol. Moral.,* I, 557; Woywod, *HPR,* XXVIII (1928), 969.

[45] It is inconsequential to dispute the date of the close of the Patristic era. Any Catholic writer not included in the first group, the Fathers, necessarily is included in the second.

[46] Gagnon, *La Censure,* n. 291; Blat (*Commentarium,* III, pars 2, n. 279) interprets the "*que*" in the phrase "*doctis catholicisque scriptoribus*" in the sense of "*simul.*"

[47] This practice obtained even before "*praecipue*" was inserted in the text by the codifiers. Previous to that time a *prima facie* reading of the law might have given the impression that it allowed the notes to be derived solely from Catholic writers; but it seems that notes derived from non-Catholic writers and from the profane sciences were allowed incidentally. This

Practically all the commentators require that notes of dogmatic, moral, exegetical, ascetical, etc., content are to be drawn exclusively from Catholic sources, whereas other details regarding the natural (profane) sciences, e.g., geography, ethnology, topography, archeology, history, chronology, philology, philosophy, etc., could be taken from the writings of any scholar irrespective of his religion.[48] Were a Catholic translator to draw notes on faith and morals from Catholic and non-Catholic writers promiscuously, his attitude might easily be mistaken for a compromise with non-Catholic religions. Tummulo-Iorio allow incidental notes from non-Catholics, even on faith and morals, but only with a view to their refutation.[49]

Nothing is determined concerning the passages to which the notes are to be appended. Obscure and difficult passages require explanation. It is left to the judgment of the translator to select these passages, and it is left to the judgment of the censor whether the translator has satisfied this need.

(5) SMALLER PARTS OF THE BIBLE

Canon 1391 fails to include the phrase "*earumque partes*" for the Sacred Scriptures as canon 1390 does for the liturgical books. Still, it is beyond doubt that each and every book of the Bible, even the shortest, is contemplated in the canon. Smaller parts of the Bible (i.e., the parts smaller than an individual book) printed separately or in other books (e.g., prayerbooks) may be edited without notes and without the special vigilance of the bishop. They are governed by the ordinary rules of censorship,[50] as now contained in canon 1385, § 1, 1°. There has been no change in the

practice was recognized by Pennacchi, *ASS,* XXX (1897–1898), 184, and *Theol. Mechlin.*, p. 205.

[48] Pernicone, *Prohibition*, p. 144; De Meester, *Compendium,* III, pars 1, n. 1348; Pennacchi, *ASS,* XXX (1897–1898), 184; Ubach, *Theol. Moral.*, I, 557; Coronata, *Institutiones*, II, n. 956, 5°; Augustine, *Admin. Law*, p. 448–449; Angelus-Nicolaus, *Manuale*, n. 558; Beste, *Introductio*, p. 684; *Theol. Mechlin.*, p. 205; Nevin, *ACR,* II (1925), 51; Marc-Gestermann-Raus, *Institutiones*, I, 856; Jombart, *DDC,* III, col. 164; Bouscaren-Ellis, *Canon Law*, p. 709; Ferreres, *Institutiones*, II, n. 388.

[49] *De Censuris*, n. 1022 (3).

[50] Vermeersch, *De Prohibitione*, n. 71, 6°.

earlier law. Such smaller parts are vernacular editions of the psalter,[51] certain psalms,[52] pericopes of the epistles and gospels of the liturgical year,[53] also the special editions of the epistles and gospels to be read to the faithful at Sunday Masses,[54] versicles and chapters,[55] parts of historical books, and even an entire historical book, e.g., Tobias.[56]

The reasons advanced for these exceptions are the following: the piety of the faithful,[57] custom,[58] or other special reasons.[59]

---

[51] Ubach, *Theol. Moral.*, I, 557; Ferreres, *Institutiones*, II, n. 388.

[52] *Theol. Mechlin.*, p. 206.

[53] Blat, *Commentarium*, III, pars 2, n. 279; Ubach, *Theol. Moral.*, I, 557; Noldin-Schmitt, *Summa*, II, n. 701; *Theol. Mechlin.*, p. 206; Coronata, *Institutiones*, II, n. 956, 5o; Sipos, *Enchiridion*, p. 714 (19); Ayrinhac, *Admin. Legisl.*, p. 284; Ferreres, *Institutiones*, II, n. 388, 4o; Wernz, *Ius Decretalium*, III, pars 1, n. 111 (58); Laurentius, *Institutiones*, n. 629 (2); Gagnon, *La Censure*, n. 291 (59); Vermeersch-Creusen, *Epitome*, II, n. 726; 6o; Wernz-Vidal, *Ius Canonicum*, IV, pars 2, n. 711; Jombart, *DDC*, III, col. 164; Marc-Gestermann-Raus, *Institutiones*, I, 856; Bouscaren-Ellis, *Canon Law*, p. 709.

[54] De Meester (*Compendium*, III, pars 1, n. 1348) allows pericopes in prayerbooks, but not in separate editions. Woywod stated that this practice is permitted, and that the Holy See has raised no objection to it—*HPR*, XXVIII (1928), 968–969.

However, it must be noted that the text from which this special translation is made must be the Latin Vulgate, and not the original Hebrew or Greek. Cf. the decision of the Pontifical Biblical Commission, 30 apr. 1934—*AAS*, XXVI (1934), 315.

[55] Blat, *Commentarium*, III, pars 2, n. 279.

[56] Périès, *L'Index*, p. 83; Moureau, *Législation*, p. 49; Marc-Gestermann-Raus, *Institutiones*, I, 856; Jombart, *DDC*, III, col. 164; Hurley, *Commentary*, p. 76; Boudinhon, *Nouv. Législ.*, p. 109; Coronata, *Institutiones*, II, n. 956, 5o; Blat, *Commentarium*, III, pars 2, n. 279; *Theol. Mechlin.*, p. 206; Vermeersch, *De Prohibitione*, n. 71, 6o; Wernz, *Ius Decretalium*, III, pars 1, n. 111 (58); Wernz-Vidal, *Ius Canonicum*, IV, pars 2, n. 711; Vermeersch-Creusen, *Epitome*, II, n. 726, 6o; Gagnon, *La Censure*, n. 291 (59); Noldin-Schmitt, *Summa*, II, n. 701; De Meester, *Compendium*, III, pars 1, n. 1348.

[57] Ferreres, *Institutiones*, II, n. 388, 4o; Coronata, *Institutiones*, II, n. 956, 5o; De Meester, *Compendium*, III, pars i, n. 1348; Marc-Gestermann-Raus, *Institutiones*, I, 856; Pernicone, *Prohibition*, p. 144; Woywod, *HPR*, XXVIII (1928), 968–969; Vermeersch, *De Prohibitione*, n. 71, 6o; Vermeersch-Creusen, *Epitome*, II, n. 726, 6o; Ubach, *Theol. Moral.*, I, 557; Laurentius, *Institutiones*, n. 629, (2); Gagnon, *La Censure*, n. 236.

[58] The following assume that the custom is quite general: Beste, *Intro-*

As mentioned above, the writer regards paraphrases of the Bible as treatises, and not as translations in the proper sense. The same would hold for Bible histories, if the text is considerably altered by the translator or editor.

(6) PROHIBITION

Canon 1399, 5°, states that the translations of the Bible are *ipso iure* prohibited if they are edited contrary to the prescriptions of canon 1391.[60] Hence, a translation of the whole Bible, or of any book of the Bible, if published without the approval, either pontifical or episcopal, is prohibited even though the translation itself be faithful, the notes reliable, and the whole version otherwise acceptable.[61] Similarly, a translation which lacks notes and fails to have apostolic approval is a prohibited version. The version is not prohibited merely if the notes are meager, somewhat faulty, etc. The prohibition means that the book may not be edited, read, kept, sold, translated or communicated to another in any way without the proper permission.[62]

The author [translator] and editor of a prohibited version of the Bible *ipso facto* incurs an excommunication, which however is not reserved for its absolution (canon 2318, § 2). The censure is

---

ductio, p. 684; Ayrinhac, *Admin. Legisl.*, p. 284; Gagnon, *La Censure*, n. 291 (5); Woywod, *HPR*, XXVIII (1928), 968; Noldin-Schmitt, *Summa*, II, n. 701; *Theol. Mechlin.*, p. 206. The following speak of the custom as existing in their own country: De Meester, *Compendium*, III, pars 1, n. 1348; Genicot-Salsmans, *Institutiones*, I, n. 453; Van Coillie, *Commentaria*, p. 44. The following admit the valid claim inherent in custom wherever the custom exists: Vermeersch, *De Prohibitione*, n. 71, 6°; Vermeersch-Creusen, *Epitome*, II, n. 726, 6°; Coronata, *Institutiones*, II, n. 956, 5°; Blat, *Commentarium*, III, pars 2, n. 279; Claeys Bouuaert-Simenon, *Manuale*, III, n. 185; Tummulo-Iorio, *De Censuris*, n. 1022, 5°; Bouscaren-Ellis, *Canon Law*, p. 709.

[59] Coronata, *Institutiones*, II, n. 956, 5°; De Meester, *Compendium*, III, pars 1, n. 1348; Wernz, *Ius Decretalium*, III, pars 1, n. 111 (58). The latter two commentators mention the use of such books in schools.

[60] A parallel canon, 1399, 1°, enjoins the same prohibition for translations of the Scriptures made by non-Catholics.

[61] *Theol. Mechlin.*, p. 205; De Meester, *Compendium*, III, pars 1, n. 1348.

[62] This canon, 1398, has been treated *ex professo* by Pernicone, *Prohibition*, pp. 142–143.

not incurred until the version is printed, and then only if the version is printed without permission.[63] The censure mentioned in canon 2318, § 2, is incurred for the printing of the Scripture in any vernacular language, even though the canon itself does not mention the translations explicitly.[64] It is to be remembered that for the incurring of this penalty the ordinary conditions for the commission of a delict must be present, especially in regard to the gravity of the matter. To be grave matter, the translation must constitute a book, or at least a booklet in the ordinary acceptance of the term,[65] and not in the Scriptural sense of the term, e.g., the book of Nahum, which at the most is only two or three pages long.

(7) SUMMARY

Canon 1391 states that translations of the Sacred Scriptures in the vernacular may not be printed unless they have been approved by the Holy See, or unless they are published under the vigilance of the bishops and are provided with notes taken principally from the Fathers of the Church and from learned, Catholic writers. The canon is concerned only with translations of the Bible, either the whole or any part, into a modern vernacular language, from any ancient text. Commentaries, etc., are not governed by this canon.

The approval is given either by the Holy See or by one of the bishops mentioned in canon 1385, § 2. Whoever grants the approval first performs the censorship. Translations approved by

---

[63] Cappello, *De Censuris* (3. ed., Taurinorum: Marietti, 1933), n. 399; Claeys Bouuaert-Simenon, *Manuale*, III, 376; Vermeersch-Creusen, *Epitome*, III, n. 517; Coronata, *Institutiones*, IV, n. 1876; Woywod, *Commentary*, II, n. 1406; Cocchi, *Commentarium*, VIII, *De Delictis et Poenis* (1. ed., Taurinorum Augustae: Marietti, 1925), n. 145; Beste, *Introductio*, p. 939; De Meester, *Compendium*, III, pars 1, n. 1387; Cerato, *Censurae Vigentes Ipso Facto a Codice Iuris Canonici Excerptae* (2. ed., Patavii, 1921), p. 71; Salucci, *Il Diritto Penale*, II, n. 36; Aertnys-Damen, *Theol. Moral.*, II, n. 1075; Wernz-Vidal, *Ius Canonicum*, VII, n. 409.

[64] Cappello, *loc. cit.;* Claeys Bouuaert-Simenon, *loc. cit.;* Vermeersch-Creusen, *loc. cit.;* Coronata, *loc. cit.;* Woywod, *loc. cit.;* Cocchi, *loc. cit.;* Beste, *loc. cit.;* De Meester, *loc. cit.;* Cerato, *loc. cit.*

[65] Cappello, *loc. cit.;* Cerato, *loc. cit.;* De Meester, *loc. cit.;* Tummulo-Iorio, *De Censuris*, n. 967.

Rome need not have notes; all other translations must have them. The chief merits of a translation are fidelity, lucidity, elegance; the chief merits of notes are their fidelity, clarity, brevity. The bishop exercises vigilance by entrusting the censorship to a qualified expert who censors the translation regarding its doctrinal and linguistic fidelity to the text from which it is taken (without sacrifice of the doctrinal prerogatives of the Vulgate edition), as well as regarding the suitability of the notes.

Notes are explanatory comments on particular passages. They serve to clarify the text, to forestall errors, etc., by presenting the traditional interpretation of the Fathers or other Catholic writers either verbatim or in an edited form. The translator may use his discretion regarding the number of notes, as well as regarding their place on the page or in the book. Notes on faith and morals must be taken exclusively from Catholics, whereas other details if borrowed from the natural sciences, may be taken from non-Catholics.

Translations of parts of the Bible smaller than an individual book, e.g. the psalter, the epistles and gospels of the liturgical year, etc., or even certain individual historical books, e. g. Tobias, may be printed separately or in prayerbooks without notes and without the vigilance of the bishops. They are governed by the ordinary rules of censorship, and their publication is allowed by reason of custom, in consideration of the piety of the faithful, or for other special reasons.

Translations of the Bible are prohibited if they are not published in conformity with the prescriptions of canon 1391. The editors and translators who print a prohibited version incur an excommunication. But the act of absolving a penitent from this excommunication is not of a reserved character.

CONCLUSIONS

1. The special classes of books enumerated in canons 1387–1391 may not be published without the permission of the Holy See. Canons 1387, 1388 and 1389 treat merely of the obtaining of the requisite permission for their publication. These canons are silent about the performance of censorship. It is a general rule that the censorship is reserved to the authority to whom the permission for the publication is reserved. However, in certain instances the Holy See may grant a conditional permission. This will take effect if and when the work passes the censorship of the local ordinary.

2. Canons 1390 and 1391 deal with the question of an approval, and not with that of a permission. The approval also presupposes a censorship on the part of the authority to whom the approval is reserved.

3. The censorship mentioned in canon 1390 is not doctrinal in character. It is concerned only with an investigation of the conformity in the text of a proffered edition to the text of an approved edition. The attestation regarding the needed conformity is an automatic guarantee of the doctrinal orthodoxy of the proffered edition.

4. It is no longer required that an author make a protestation of submission to the judgment of the Church at the beginning of a biography of a Servant of God. The decree prescribing this formality, enacted by Pope Urban VIII, was abrogated by Pope Leo XIII in his Constitution "*Officiorum ac munerum.*"

5. Canon 1388, § 1, which allows the local ordinary to permit the publication of indulgences (save those whose publication is reserved to the Holy See by § 2) is an explicit statement of the law which is implicitly contained in canon 1385, § 1, 2°.

6. Remembrance cards printed as souvenirs of religious occasions may be printed without the permission and censorship of the local ordinary, even though they contain a few indulgenced prayers or ejaculations. This well-established custom is permissible in view of the fact that it connotes a private printing rather than

a true publication. It is entirely beside the point to argue, as most of the authors do, that these cards are not leaflets. The favor of this exception is applicable even for the printing of leaflets under the contemplated circumstances.

7. A bishop exercises the vigilance required of him in canon 1391 by entrusting the censorship of a translation of the Sacred Scripture to a qualified expert. The latter will censor the version regarding its doctrinal and linguistic fidelity to the text from which the translation is made, but he must at the same time always respect and honor the doctrinal supremacy of the Vulgate. He will also investigate the suitability of the notes.

BIBLIOGRAPHY

SOURCES

Acta Apostolicae Sedis, Commentarium Officiale, Romae, 1909—

Acta Sanctae Sedis, 41 vols., Romae, 1865–1908.

Bullarii Romani Continuatio Summorum Pontificum, 19 vols., Prati, 1756–1883.

Bullarum Diplomatum et Privilegiorum Sanctorum Romanorum Pontificum Taurinensis Editio, 24 vols. et Appendix, Augustae Taurinorum, 1857–1872.

Caeremoniale Episcoporum, Parisiis, 1860.

Canones et Decreta Concilii Tridentini ex editione romana a. MDCCC-XXXIV repetiti, ed. Neapolitana, Neapoli, 1859.

Codex Iuris Canonici Pii X Pontificis Maximi iussu digestus Benedicti Papae XV auctoritate promulgatus, Romae, Typis Polyglottis Vaticanis, 1917.

Codex pro Postulatoribus Causarum Beatificationis et Canonizationis, editio quarta ad novi Iuris Canonici normas exacta cura postulationis generalis Ordinis Fratrum Minorum, Romae: Libreria del Collegio S. Antonio, 1929.

Codicis Iuris Canonici Fontes, cura Emi Petri Card. Gasparri editi, 9 vols., Romae [postea Civitate Vaticana]: Typis Polyglottis Vaticanis, 1923–1939 (Vols. VII–IX, ed. cura et studio Emi Iustiniani Card. Serédi).

Collectanea Sacrae Congregationis de Propaganda Fide, Romae, 1893.

Concilii Plenarii Baltimorensis II, in Ecclesia Metropolitana Baltimorensi, a die VII. ad diem XXI. Octobris, A. D. MDCCCLXVI, habiti, et a Sede Apostolica recogniti, Acta et Decreta, 2. ed., Baltimorae, 1894.

Corpus Iuris Canonici, ed. Lipsiensis secunda, post Aemilii Richteri curas . . . instruxit Aemilius Friedberg, 2 vols., Lipsiae, 1879–1881.

Decreta Authentica Congregationis Sacrorum Rituum ex actis eiusdem collecta eiusque auctoritate promulgata sub auspiciis SS. Domini nostri Leonis Papae XIII, 5 vols. et 2 Appendices, Romae, 1898–1927.

Decreta Authentica Sacrae Congregationis Indulgentiis Sacrisque Reliquiis praepositae ab anno 1668 ad annum 1882 edita, iussu et auctoritate Sanctissimi D. N. Leonis PP. XIII, Ratisbonae-Neo-Eboraci-Cincinnatii, 1883.

Falise, J. B., *Sacrae Congregationis Indulgentiarum Resolutiones Authenticae,* Lovanii, 1862.

Index Librorum Prohibitorum iuxta exemplar Romanum, iussu Ssmi Domini Nostri Leonis XIII Pontificis Maximi editum anno MDCCCLXXXIV editio novissima, Mechliniae, 1893.

Ius pontificium de Propaganda Fide, ed. R. de Martinis, pars I, 7 vols., Romae, 1888–1897; pars II, Romae, 1909.

Martyrologium Romanum Gregorii Papae XIII iussu editum Urbani VIII et Clementis X auctoritate recognitum ac deinde anno MDCCXLIX Benedicti XIV opera ac studio emendatum et auctum. Secunda post typicam editio iuxta primam a typica editionem anno MDCCCCXXII a Benedicto Papa XV adprobatum propriis recentium sanctorum officiorumque elogiis expleta Sacrae Rituum Congregationis curis impressa Civitate Vaticana, Typis Polyglottis Vaticanis, 1930.

Memoriale Rituum, Ritual for small Churches, issued by Pope Benedict XIII, and revised by authority of Pope Benedict XV, ed. by Rev. Bartholomew Eustace, New York: Wagner, [1935].

Missale Romanum ex decreto Sacrosancti Concilii Tridentini restitutum, S. Pii V Pontificis Maximi iussu editum, aliorum Pontificum cura recognitum, a Pio X reformatum et Ssmi D. N. Benedicti XV auctoritate vulgatum, Ratisbonae, 1925.

Pii IX Pontificis Maximi Acta, 9 vols., Romae, 1854–1878.

Pontificale Romanum, Summorum Pontificum iussu editum, a Benedicto XIV et Leone XIII Pont. Max. recognitum et castigatum, Ratisbonae, 1908.

Preces et Pia Opera in favorem omnium Christifidelium vel quorumdam coetuum personarum indulgentiis ditata et opportune recognita, Civitate Vaticana, Typis Polyglottis Vaticanis, 1938.

Prinzivalli, A., *Resolutiones seu Decreta Authentica S. Congregationis Indulgentiis Sacrisque Reliquiis praepositae ab anno 1668 ad annum 1861 accurate collecta,* Romae, 1862.

Psalterium Breviarii Romani cum excerptis e communi Sanctorum secundum novam e textibus primigeniis interpretationem latinam Pii Papae XII auctoritate editum, editio iuxta typicam vaticanam, Novi Eboraci: Benziger Bros., 1945.

Raccolta di Orazioni e Pie Opere per le quali sono state concedute dai Sommi Pontefici le S. Indulgenze, 7. ed., Romae: Typografia Perego-Salvioni, 1831.

Raccolta, The or, *Collection of Prayers and Good Works to which the Sovereign Pontiffs have attached Holy Indulgences, published by order of His Holiness, Pope Pius IX,* translation authorized and approved by the Sacred Congregation of Holy Indulgences, Philadelphia, 1881.

———, *Prayers and Devotions enriched with indulgences authorized by the Holy See,* New York, edited and translated by J. Christopher and C. Spence, New York: Benziger Bros., 1943.

———, *A Collection of Indulgenced Prayers to which the Supreme Roman Pontiffs for all Christians or for definite organizations of persons have attached indulgences from the year 1899 to the year 1928,* tr. by A. Breen, Milwaukee, Keystone Printing Service, 1931.

Rituale Romanum Pauli V Pontificis Maximi iussu editum aliorumque

Pontificum cura recognitum atque auctoritate Sanctissimi D. N. Pii Papae XI ad normam Codicis Iuris Canonici accomodatum, 6. ed. post typicam, Turonibus, Mame, 1936.

Schneider, J., *Rescripta Authentica Sacrae Congregationis Indulgentiis Sacrisque Reliquiis praepositae necnon Summaria Indulgentiarum,* Ratisbonae—Neo Eboraci—Cincinnati, 1885.

Sylloge praecipuorum documentorum recentium Summorum Pontificum et S. Congregationis de Propaganda Fide necnon aliarum SS. Congregationum Romanarum ad usum missionariorum, Civitate Vaticana; Typis Polyglottis Vaticanis, 1939.

REFERENCE WORKS

Acta Canonizationum Quibus Sanctissimus Dominus Noster Pius Papa XI ab anno sacro 1933 ad annum 1935 Beatis Sanctorum Caelitum Honores Decrevit, cura Alfonsi Carinci Collecta, Insulae Liri: Macioce et Pisani, 1939.

Aertnys, Josephus-Damen, C. A., *Theologia Moralis secundum doctrinam S. Alfonsi de Ligorio Doctoris Ecclesiae,* 14. ed., 2 vols., Taurinorum Augustae: Marietti, 1944.

Angelus a SS. Corde Jesu—Nicolaus a Pmo Corde Mariae, *Manuale Juris Communis Regularium et Specialis Carmelitarum Discalceatorum,* Burgis: Typ. "El Monte Carmelo," 1929.

Arndt, Augustinus, *De Libris Prohibitis Commentarii,* Ratisbonae, 1895.

Arregui, Antonius, *Summarium Theologiae Moralis,* 13. ed., Westminster: Newman Bookshop, 1944.

Augustine, Charles, *A Commentary on the New Code of Canon Law,* 8 vols., Vol. IV, 1920; Vol. VI, 1921; Vol. VII, 1921, St. Louis, 1918–1922.

Ayrinhac, H. A., *Administrative Legislation in the New Code of Canon Law,* New York: Longmans, Green & Co., 1930.

Baart, Peter, *Legal Formulary,* 5. ed., New York, 1898.

Bangen, Johann H., *Die römische Kurie, ihregegenwärtige Zusammensetzung und ihr Geschäftsgang. Nach mehrjähiger eigener Anschauung dargestellt,* Münster, 1854.

Benedictus XIV, *De Servorum Dei Beatificatione, et Beatorum Canonizatione,* in *Opera Omnia,* 17 vols., Prati, 1839–1846.

Beringer, Franz-Steinen, P., *Die Ablässe, ihr Wesen und Gebrauch,* 15. ed., 2 vols., Paderborn, 1916–1921.

Berutti, Christophorus, *Institutiones Iuris Canonici,* 6 vols., [Vol. V sub praelo], Taurini-Romae: Marietti, 1936–1943.

Beste, Udalricus, *Introductio in Codicem,* 2. ed., Collegeville: St. John's Abbey Press, 1944.

Blat, Albertus, *Commentarium Textus Codicis Iuris Canonici,* 5 vols. in 6, Vol. III, pars 2, 1923, Romae: Ex Typographia Pontificia in Instituto Pii IX, 1919–1927.

Boudinhon, A., *La Nouvelle Législation de l'Index,* 2. ed., Paris, 1925.

Bouix, D., *De Iure Liturgico,* Parisiis, 1873.

Bouscaren, T. Lincoln-Ellis, Adam C., *Canon Law, A Text and Commentary,* Milwaukee: Bruce Publ. Co., 1946.

Bouscaren, T. Lincoln, *The Canon Law Digest,* 2 vols., Milwaukee: Bruce Publ. Co., 1934–1943.

Cance, Adrien, *Le Code de Droit Canonique,* 2. ed., 3 vols., Paris: Librairie Lecoffre, 1929.

Cappello, Felix M., *De Censuris,* 3. ed., Taurinorum Augustae: Marietti, 1933.

———, *De Curia Romana,* 2. vol., Romae, 1911–1912.

Catholic Encyclopedia, The, 15 vols., Index and Supplements, New York, 1907–1922.

Cerato, Prosdocimus, *Censurae Vigentes Ipso Facto a Codice Iuris Canonici Excerptae,* 2. ed., Patavii, 1921.

Cicognani, Amleto, *Canon Law,* tr. O'Hara-Brennan, Philadelphia, Dolphin Press, 1934.

Claeys Bouuaert, F.-Simenon, G., *Manuale Juris Canonici,* 3 vols., Vols. I and III, 4. ed., 1934, Vol. II, 2. ed., 1935, Gandae et Leodii: Apud Seminaria, 1934–1935.

Cocchi, Guidus, *Commentarium in Codicem Iuris Canonici ad usum Scholarum,* 8 vols. in 5, Vol. VI, 2. ed., 1927, Taurinorum Augustae: Marietti, 1920–1930.

Cogliolo, Pietro, *Manuale delle Fonti del Diritto Romano,* 2. ed., Torino, 1911.

Coronata, Mattheus Conte a, *Institutiones Iuris Canonici,* 5 vols., Taurini: Marietti, 1928–1936.

———, *Interpretatio Authentica Codicis Iuris Canonici et circa ipsum Sanctae Sedis Iurisprudentia 1916–1940,* Taurini-Romae: Marietti, 1940.

De Meester, A., *Juris Canonici et Juris Canonico-Civilis Compendium,* 2. ed., 3 vols. in 4, Brugis: Societas Sancti Augustini, 1921–1928.

Dictionnaire de Droit Canonique, Paris: Letouzey et Ané, 1935—

Duchesne, Louis, *Origines du culte chrétien,* 5. ed., Paris, 1925.

Dufourcq, Albert, *Études sur les Gesta Martyrum Romains,* Paris, 1900.

Dziob, Michael W., *The Sacred Congregation for the Oriental Church,* The Catholic University of America Canon Law Studies, No. 142, Washington, D. C.: The Catholic University of America Press, 1945.

Ferreres, Joannes, *Institutiones Canonicae iuxta Novissimum Codicem,* 2. ed., 2 vols., Barcinone, 1920.

Fortescue, Adrian-O'Connell, J., *The Ceremonies of the Roman Rite Described,* 6. ed., London: Burns, Oates and Washbourne, Ltd., 1937.

Gagnon, Edouard, *Le Censure des Livres,* Les Theses Canoniques de Laval, n. 3, Quebec: Université Laval, 1945.

Gallik, George A., *The Rights and Duties of Bishops Regarding Diocesan Sisterhoods,* St. Paul: The Wanderer Printing Co., 1939.

Genicot, Eduardus-Salsmans, I., *Institutiones Theologiae Moralis,* 14. ed., 2 vols., Buenos Aires: Dedebec, Ediciones Desclee, De Brouwer, 1939.

Grannan, Charles P., *A General Introduction to the Bible,* 4 vols., St. Louis, 1921.

Haring, Johann B., *Grundzüge des katholischen Kirchenrechts,* 2. ed., 2 vols. Graz, 1924.

Heymans, A., *De ecclesiastica librorum aliorumque scriptorum in Belgia prohibitione disquisitio,* Bruxellis, 1849.

Hilling, Nicholas, *Procedure at the Roman Curia* (a concise and practical handbook, translated and adapted with the author's consent), New York: J. F. Wagner, 1907.

Hollweck, Joseph, *Das kirchliche Bücherverbot,* 2. ed., Mainz, 1897.

Hurley, T., *A Commentary on the Present Index Legislation,* Dublin, 1907.

Koestler, Rudolf, *Wörterbuch zum Codex Iuris Canonici,* München: F. Pustet, 1927–1929.

Laurentius, Iosephus, *Institutiones Iuris Ecclesiastici,* 3. ed., Friburgi in B., 1914.

Lega, Michael, *Praelectiones in Textum Iuris Canonici de Iudiciis Ecclesiasticis in Scholis Pont. Sem. Rom. Habitae,* 4 vols., Romae, 1896–1901.

Lehmkuhl, Augustinus, *Theologia Moralis,* 12. ed., 2 vols., Friburgi, 1914.

Lépicier, Alexis H. M., *Indulgences, Their Origin, Nature and Development,* 3. ed., London: Burns, Oates and Washbourne, Ltd., 1928.

Lexikon für Theologie und Kirche, 10 vols., Freiburg im B.: B. Herder, 1930–1938.

Lijdsman, Bernardus, *Introductio in Jus Canonicum cum uberiori fontium studio,* 2 vols. in 1, Hilversium in Hollandia, 1924–1929.

Marc, Cl.-Gestermann, Fr. X.-Raus, J. B., *Institutiones Morales Alphonsianae seu Doctoris Ecclesiae S. Alphonsi Mariae de Ligorio Doctrina Moralis ad usum Scholarum accomodata,* 18. ed., 2 vols., Lugduni: E. Vitte, 1927.

Martin, Michael, *The Roman Curia,* New York, 1913.

Maurel, Antoine, *Die Ablässe, ihr Wesen und ihr Gebrauch,* Paderborn, 1860.

Michiels, Gommarus, *Normae Generales Iuris Canonici,* 2 vols., Lublin: Universitas Catholica, 1929.

Migne, Jacques Paul, *Patrologiae Cursus Completus, Series Latina,* 221 vols., Parisiis, 1844–1864.

Mocchegiani, P., *Collectio Indulgentiarum theologice, canonice, ac historice digesta,* Quaracchi, 1897.

Monin, Arthur, *De Curia Romana,* Lovanii, 1912.

Moretti, A., *Caeremoniale iuxta ritum romanum,* 4 vols., Taurini-Romae: Marietti, 1936–1939.

Moureau, H., *La Nouvelle législation de l'Index,* Lille, 1898.

Muñiz, T., *Procedimientos Eclesiásticos,* 2. ed., 3 vols., Sevilla, 1925.

Musser, Benjamin, *Kyrie Eleison,* Westminster: Newman Bookshop, 1946.

Noldin, H.-Schmitt, A., *Summa Theologiae Moralis,* 3 vols., Vol. II, 27. ed., 1941, Oeniponte-Lipsiae: F. Rauch, 1941–1942.

Noval, Josephus, *Commentarium Codicis Iuris Canonici,* lib. IV, *De Processibus,* 2 vols., Augustae Taurinorum: Marietti, 1920–1932.

Ojetti, Benedictus, *De Romana Curia,* Romae, 1910.

Paulus, Nikolaus, *Geschichte des Ablasses im Mittelalter, vom Ursprung bis zur Mitte des 14 Jahrhunderts,* 2 vols., Paderborn, 1922–1923.

Pejška, Iosephus, *Ius Canonicum Religiosorum,* 3. ed., Friburgi in B.: B. Herder, 1927.

Périès, G., *L'Index: commentaire de la constitution apostolique " Officiorum,"* Paris, 1898.

Pernicone, Joseph M., *The Ecclesiastical Prohibition of Books,* The Catholic University of America Canon Law Studies No. 72, Washington, D. C.: The Catholic University of America, 1932.

Phillips, George, *Kirchenrecht,* 7 vols., Regensburg, 1845–1872.

Piscetta, A.-Gennaro, A., *Elementa Theologiae Moralis ad Codicem Iuris Canonici Exacta,* 5. ed., 7 vols. in 6, Torino: Societa Editrice, 1938–1943; Vol. II, 5. ed., 1942.

Prümmer, Dominicus, *Manuale Iuris Canonici in usum Scholarum,* 3. ed., Friburgi Brisgoviae, 1922.

Regatillo, Eduardus, *Institutiones Iuris Canonici,* 2 vols., Santander: Sal Terrae, 1941–1942.

Reiffenstuel, Anacletus, *Ius Canonicum Universum,* 5 vols. in 7, Parisiis, 1864–1870.

Roberti, Franciscus, *De Processibus,* 2 vols. in 1, Romae, 1926.

Romita, Fiorenzo, *Ius Musicae Liturgicae,* Taurini: Marietti, 1936.

Sabetti, Aloysius-Barrett, Timotheus, *Compendium Theologiae Moralis,* 34. ed., Neo Eboraci-Cincinnati: F. Pustet, 1939.

Salaville, Sévérien, *An Introduction to the Study of Eastern Liturgies,* adapted from the French by John Barton, London: Sands & Co., 1938.

Salucci, Raffaele, *Il Diritto Penale Secondo Il Codice di Diritto Canonico,* 2 vols., Subiaco: Typografia dei Monasteri, 1926–1930.

Sartori, Cosmas, *Enchiridion canonicum seu Sanctae Sedis responsiones post Codicem Iuris Canonici datae iuxta canonum Codicis ordinem digestae notulisque ornatae* (1917–1944), 7. ed., Romae: Ex Typographia Augustiniana, 1944.

Schmalzgrueber, Franciscus, *Ius Ecclesiasticum Universum,* 5 vols. in 12, Romae, 1843–1845.

Schneider, Philip, *Die neuen Büchergesetze der Kirche,* Mainz, 1900.

Seraphinus a Loiano, *Institutiones Theologiae Moralis ad normam Iuris Canonici,* 4 vols., Vol. II, 1935, Taurini: Marietti, 1934–1940.

Shearer, Donald C., *Pontificia Americana: A Documentary History of the Catholic Church in the United States (1784–1884),* The Catholic University of America Studies in American Church History, Vol. XV, Washington, D. C.: The Catholic University of America, 1933.

Sipos, Stephanus, *Enchiridion Iuris Canonici,* Pécs: Ex Typographia "Haladás R. T.," 1926.

Stella, Franciscus, *Institutiones Liturgicae in Seminariorum usum,* 2. ed., Romae, 1895.

Theologia Mechliniensis: Tractatus de Censuris, Casibus Reservatis, Irregularitatibus et Libris Prohibitis ad usum alumnorum Seminarii Archiepiscopalis Mechliniensis, 3. ed., Mechliniae, 1906.

Tummulo, R.-Iorio, T. A., *Compendium Theologiae Moralis,* 5. ed., 2 vols., 1934–1935, Suppl. [*De Censuris, Prohibitione Librorum, Irregularitatibus, Indulgentiis*], Neapoli: M. D'Auria, 1936.

Ubach, Josephus, *Theologia Moralis Codici Juris Canonici accomodatum,* 2. ed., 2 vols., Bonis Auris: Sociedad San Miguel, 1935.

Ubaldi, Ubaldus, *Introductio in Sacram Scripturam ad usum Scholarum Pont. Seminarii Romani et Collegii Urbani de Propaganda Fide,* 4. ed., 3 vols., Romae, 1891.

Van Coillie, Constantinus, *Commentaria in constitutionem Ssm̃i Dñi Leonis XIII "Officiorum ac munerum,"* Brugis, 1899.

Van Hove, *Commentarium Lovaniense in Codicem Iuris Canonici editum a Magistris et Doctoribus Universitatis Lovaniensis* Vol. I, tom. 1, *Prolegomena ad Codicem Iuris Canonici,* 2. ed., Mechliniae-Romae, H. Dessain, 1945.

Vermeersch, Arthurus, *De Prohibitione et Censura Librorum Dissertatio canonico-moralis,* 4. ed., Romae, 1906.

Vermeersch, A.,-Creusen, J., *Epitome Iuris Canonici cum commentariis ad scholas et ad usum privatum,* 4. ed., 3 vols., Mechliniae-Romae: H. Dessain, 1929–1931.

Wernz, Franciscus, *Ius Decretalium,* 2. ed., 6 vols. in 10, Prati, 1906–1913.

Wernz, Franciscus-Vidal, Petrus, *Ius Canonicum ad normam Codicis exactum,* 7 vols. in 8, Vol. IV pars 2, 1935; Vol. VI, 1927; Vol. VII, 1937; Romae: Apud Aedes Universitatis Gregorianae, 1923–1938.

Woywod, Stanislaus, *A Practical Commentary on the Code of Canon Law,* 3. ed., 2 vols., New York: J. Wagner, 1929.

Woywod, Stanislaus, *Canonical Decisions of the Holy See,* New York: J. Wagner, 1933.

Wuest, Joseph-Mullaney, Thomas, *Matters Liturgical,* 5. ed., New York-Cincinnati, F. Pustet, 1938.

Zaccaria, F. A., *Storia polemica delle proibizioni de' libri,* Romae, 1777.

ARTICLES

Boudinhon, A., "Les Nouvelles Règles sur l'Interdiction et la Censure des Livres"—*Le Canoniste Contemporain,* XX (1897), 129–137, 206–215, 297–310, 432–447, 665–677, XXI (1898), 16–35; 129–149, 241–254, 305–316, 382–390, 541–563, 656–668.

Cadène, "Collectio decretorum responsorumque S. Officii,"—*Analecta Ecclesiastica,* Revue Romaine, II (1894), 318–321, 360–362, 407–412,

493–495; III (1895), 32–33, 79–82, 115–122, 167–169, 262–263, 297–302, 352–354, 457–465, 494–498; IV (1896), 76–83, 123–128, 179–192, 273–277, 361–366, 420–421, 462–465.

Dausend, H., "Pontificale Romanum"—*Lexikon für Theologie und Kirche,* VII (1936), col. 371–373.

Desjardins, S., "La Nouvelle Constitution apostolique sur l'Index"—*Études religieuses des PP. Jesuites,* LXX (1897), 737–747; LXXI (1897), 208–219, 361–376.

Gagnon, Edouard, "La Lecture des livres par les fideles"—*Semaine Religieuse de Quebec,* LV (1944), 246–253.

G[énnari], M. C., "Circa La Nuova Disciplina Sulla Proibizione e Sulla Censura de'Libri"—*Il Monitore Ecclesiastico,* X, pars 1 (1897), 13–18, 33–40, 63–69, 80–86, 105–112, 132–136, 153–157.

Jombart, Emile, "Censure des Livres"—*Dictionnaire de Droit Canonique,* III, fasc. 13 (1938), col. 157–169.

Korolevskij, Cyril, "The Liturgical Publications of the Sacred Congregation for the Eastern Church"—*The Eastern Churches Quarterly,* VI (1945–1946), 87–96, 388–399.

Mershman, Francis, "Litany of the Saints"—*The Catholic Encyclopedia,* IX (1913), 291–292.

Nevin, J. J., "Censorship of Books"—*Australasian Catholic Record,* II (1925), 51–56.

Pennacchi, Iosephus, "In Constitutionem Apostolicam '*officiorum ac munerum*' Brevis Commentatio"—*Acta Sanctae Sedis,* XXX (1897–1898), 33–96, 161–224, 289–352, 385–416, 481–534, 535–536.

Piat, P., "Commentaire de la Constitution '*officiorum ac munerum*' de Sa Sainteté le Pape Léon XIII sur la prohibition et la censure des livres et des décrets généraux qui l'accompagnent"—*Nouvelle Revue Théologique,* XXX (1898), 44–63, 469–485, 579–599; XXXI (1899), 12–31, 131–142, 341–358, 565–584; XXXII (1900), 1–22, 131–139, 341–355, 466–479, 565–578; XXXIII (1901), 15–26, 132–145.

Santi, Angelo de, "Litany of Loreto"—*The Catholic Encyclopedia,* IX (1913), 287–290.

V[ermeersch], A[rthurus], "De Codice et de editione cantus gregoriani"—*Ius Pontificium,* XV (1935), 235.

Vermeersch, Arthurus, "Annotationes"—*Periodica,* XVIII (1929), 171.

Woywod, Stanislaus, "Law of the Code—Ecclesiastical Censorship"—*Homiletic and Pastoral Review,* XXVIII (1928), 628–631, 861–869, 966–973.

PERIODICALS

Australasian Catholic Record, Sidney, 1924—

Canoniste Contemporaine Le, Parisiis, 1878–1922; ab anno 1924–1926, *Le Canoniste.*

Eastern Churches Quarterly, The, Ramsgate, 1936—

Études religieuses des PP. Jesuites, Paris, 1856—. Ab anno 1856 ad annum 1861, *Études de théologie, de philosophie et d'histoire;* ab anno 1862 ad annum 1896, *Études religieuses, philosophiques et historiques.*

Homiletic and Pastoral Review, The, New York, 1900—

Ius Pontificium, Romae, 1921—

Jurist, The, Washington, D. C., 1941—

Monitore Ecclesiastico, Il, Romae, 1876—

Nouvelle Revue Théologique, Paris, 1869—; ab anno 1856 ad annum 1863, *Revue Théologique.*

Periodica de Religiosis et Missionariis, Brugis, 1905–1919; *Periodica de Re Canonica et Morali utili praesertim Religiosis et Missionariis*, 1920–1927; *Periodica de Re Morali, Canonica, Liturgica*, Brugis, 1927–1936; Romae, 1937—

Semaine Religieuse de Quebec, Quebec, 1899—.

ABBREVIATIONS

AAS—*Acta Apostolicae Sedis.*

ASS—*Acta Sanctae Sedis.*

BRC—*Bullarii Romani Continuatio Summorum Pontificum.*

BRT—*Bullarum Diplomatum et Privilegiorum Romanorum Pontificum Taurinensis Editio.*

CC—*Le Canoniste Contemporaine.*

DDC—*Dictionnaire de Droit Canonique.*

Decr. Auth.—*Decreta Authentica Congregationis Sacrorum Rituum.*

Decr. Auth. Indulg.—*Decreta Authentica Sacrae Congregationis Indulgentiis Sacrisque Reliquiis praepositae.*

ECQ—*The Eastern Churches Quarterly.*

Études—*Études religieuses des PP. Jesuites.*

Fontes—*Codicis Iuris Canonici Fontes.*

HPR—*The Homiletic and Pastoral Review.*

Mansi—*Sacrorum Conciliorum Nova et Amplissima Collectio.*

Monit. Eccl.—*Il Monitore Ecclesiastico.*

NRT—*Nouvelle Revue Théologique.*

Rescr. Auth.—*Rescripta Authentica Sacrae Congregationis Indulg.* (ed. J. Schneider).

S. C. Indicis—Sacra Congregatio Indicis.

S. C. S. Off.—Suprema Congregatio Sancti Officii.

S. Poenit. Ap.—Sacra Poenitentiaria Apostolica.

S. R. C.—Sacrorum Rituum Congregatio.

ALPHABETICAL INDEX

BIOGRAPHICAL NOTE

Nathaniel Louis Sonntag was born in Sheboygan, Wisconsin, December 9, 1915. After completing his elementary education at Holy Name School, Sheboygan, he attended St. Lawrence College, Mount Calvary, Wisconsin. He entered the Capuchin Novitiate, Huntington, Indiana, in 1934, and was professed the following year. He pursued further studies at the Capuchin Clericates—Philosophy in Mary Immaculate Friary, Glenclyffe, Garrison, New York, and Theology in St. Anthony Friary, Marathon, Wisconsin. At the latter place he was ordained on June 24, 1942. He served as assistant director of the St. Bonaventure Third Order Fraternity in Detroit, Michigan, before entering the Canon Law School at the Catholic University of America in the Fall of 1944. From this School he received the degree of Baccalaureate in Canon Law in May of 1945, and the degree of Licentiate in Canon Law in June of 1946.

Canon Law Studies *

1. Freriks, Rev. Celestine A., C.PP.S., J.C.D., Religious Congregations in Their External Relations, 121 pp., 1916.
2. Galliher, Rev. Daniel M., O.P., J.C.D., Canonical Elections, 117 pp., 1917.
3. Borkowski, Rev. Aurelius L., O.F.M., J.C.D., De Confraternitatibus Ecclesiasticis, 136 pp., 1918.
4. Castillo, Rev. Cayo, J.C.D., Disertacion Historico-Canonica sobre la Potestad del Cabildo en Sede Vacante o Impedida del Vicario Capitular, 99 pp., 1919 (1918).
5. Kubelbeck, Rev. William J., S.T.B., J.C.D., The Sacred Penitentiaria and Its Relation to Faculties of Ordinaries and Priests, 129 pp., 1918.
6. Petrovits, Rev. Joseph J. C., S.T.D., J.C.D., The New Church Law on Matrimony, X-461 pp., 1919.
7. Hickey, Rev. John J., S.T.B., J.C.D., Irregularities and Simple Impediments in the New Code of Canon Law, 100 pp., 1920.
8. Klekotka, Rev. Peter J., S.T.B., J.C.D., Diocesan Consultors, 179 pp., 1920.
9. Wanenmacher, Rev. Francis, J.C.D., The Evidence in Ecclesiastical Procedure Affecting the Marriage Bond, 1920 (Printed 1935).
10. Golden, Rev. Henry Francis, J.C.D., Parochial Benefices in the New Code, IV-119 pp., 1921 (Printed 1925).
11. Koudelka, Rev. Charles J., J.C.D., Pastors, Their Rights and Duties According to the New Code of Canon Law, 211 pp., 1921.
12. Melo, Rev. Antonius, O.F.M., J.C.D., De Exemptione Regularium, X-188 pp., 1921.
13. Schaaf, Rev. Valentine Theodore, O.F.M., S.T.B., J.C.D., The Cloister, X-180 pp., 1921.
14. Burke, Rev. Thomas Joseph, S.T.D., J.C.D., Competence in Ecclesiastical Tribunals, IV-117 pp., 1922.
15. Leech, Rev. George Leo, J.C.D., A Comparative Study of the Constitution "Apostolicae Sedis" and the "Codex Juris Canonici," 179 pp., 1922.
16. Motry, Rev. Hubert Louis, S.T.D., J.C.D., Diocesan Faculties According to the Code of Canon Law, II-167 pp., 1922.
17. Murphy, Rev. George Lawrence, J.C.D., Delinquencies and Penalties in the Administration and the Reception of the Sacraments, IV-121 pp., 1923.

* From nn. 1–100 inclusive only n. 25 is still obtainable. From n. 101 onward all numbers are available except the following: 101–114, 116, 118, 120, 122, 123 and 162.

18. O'Reilly, Rev. John Anthony, S.T.B., J.C.D., Ecclesiastical Sepulture in the New Code of Canon Law, II-129 pp., 1923.
19. Michalicka, Rev. Wenceslas Cyrill, O.S.B., J.C.D., Judicial Procedure in Dismissal of Clerical Exempt Religious, 107 pp., 1923.
20. Dargin, Rev. Edward Vincent, S.T.B., J.C.D., Reserved Cases According to the Code of Canon Law, IV-103 pp., 1924.
21. Godfrey, Rev. John A., S.T.B., J.C.D., The Right of Patronage According to the Code of Canon Law, 153 pp., 1924.
22. Hagedorn, Rev. Francis Edward, J.C.D., General Legislation on Indulgences, II-154 pp., 1924.
23. King, Rev. James Ignatius, J.C.D., The Administration of the Sacraments to Dying Non-Catholics, V-141 pp., 1924.
24. Winslow, Rev. Francis Joseph, M.M., J.C.D., Vicars and Prefects Apostolic, IV-149 pp., 1924.
25. Correa, Rev. Jose Servelion, S.T.L., J.C.D., La Potestad Legislativa de la Iglesia Catolica, IV-127 pp., 1925.
26. Dugan, Rev. Henry Francis, A.M., J.C.D., The Judiciary Department of the Diocesan Curia, 87 pp., 1925.
27. Keller, Rev. Charles Frederick, S.T.B., J.C.D., Mass Stipends, 167 pp., 1925.
28. Paschang, Rev. John Linus, J.C.D., The Sacramentals According to the Code of Canon Law, 129 pp., 1925.
29. Piontek, Rev. Cyrillus, O.F.M., S.T.B., J.C.D., De Indulto Exclaustrationis necnon Saecularizationis, XIII-289 pp., 1925.
30. Kearney, Rev. Richard Joseph, S.T.B., J.C.D., Sponsors at Baptism According to the Code of Canon Law, IV-127 pp., 1925.
31. Bartlett, Rev. Chester Joseph, A.M., LL.B., J.C.D., The Tenure of Parochial Property in the United States of America, V-108 pp., 1926.
32. Kilker, Rev. Adrian Jerome, J.C.D., Extreme Unction, V-425 pp., 1926.
33. McCormick, Rev. Robert Emmett, J.C.D., Confessors of Religious, VIII-266 pp., 1926.
34. Miller, Rev. Newton Thomas, J.C.D., Founded Masses According to the Code of Canon Law, VII-93 pp., 1926.
35. Roelker, Rev. Edward G., S.T.D., J.C.D., Principles of Privilege According to the Code of Canon Law, XI-166 pp., 1926.
36. Bakalarczyk, Rev. Richardus, M.I.C., J.U.D., De Novitiatu, VIII-208 pp., 1927.
37. Pizzuti, Rev. Lawrence, O.F.M., J.U.L., De Parochis Religiosis, 1927. (Not Printed.)
38. Bliley, Rev. Nicholas Martin, O.S.B., J.C.D., Altars According to the Code of Canon Law, XIX-132 pp., 1927.
39. Brown, Mr. Brendan Francis, A.B., LL.M., J.U.D., The Canonical Juristic Personality with Special Reference to its Status in the United States of America, V-212 pp., 1927.

40. Cavanaugh, Rev. William Thomas, C.P., J.U.D., The Reservation of the Blessed Sacrament, VIII-101 pp., 1927.
41. Doheny, Rev. William J., C.S.C., A.B., J.U.D., Church Property: Modes of Acquisition, X-118 pp., 1927.
42. Feldhaus, Rev. Aloysius H., C.PP.S., J.C.D., Oratories, IX-141 pp., 1927.
43. Kelly, Rev. James Patrick, A.B., J.C.D., The Jurisdiction of the Simple Confessor, X-208 pp., 1927.
44. Neuberger, Rev. Nicholas J., J.C.D., Canon 6 or the Relation of the Codex Juris Canonici to the Preceding Legislation, V-95 pp., 1927.
45. O'Keefe, Rev. Gerald Michael, J.C.D., Matrimonial Dispensations, Powers of Bishops, Priests, and Confessors, VIII-232 pp., 1927.
46. Quigley, Rev. Joseph A. M., A.B., J.C.D., Condemned Societies, 139 pp., 1927.
47. Zaplotnik, Rev. Johannes Leo, J.C.D., De Vicariis Foraneis, X-142 pp., 1927.
48. Duskie, Rev. John Aloysius, A.B., J.C.D., The Canonical Status of the Orientals in the United States, VIII-196 pp., 1928.
49. Hyland, Rev. Francis Edward, J.C.D., Excommunication, Its Nature, Historical Development and Effects, VIII-181 pp., 1928.
50. Reinmann, Rev. Gerald Joseph, O.M.C., J.C.D., The Third Order Secular of Saint Francis, 201 pp., 1928.
51. Schenk, Rev. Francis J., J.C.D., The Matrimonial Impediments of Mixed Religion and Disparity of Cult, XVI-318 pp., 1929.
52. Coady, Rev. John Joseph, S.T.D., J.U.D., A.M., The Appointment of Pastors, VIII-150 pp., 1929.
53. Kay, Rev. Thomas Henry, J.C.D., Competence in Matrimonial Procedure, VIII-164 pp., 1929.
54. Turner, Rev. Sidney Joseph, C.P., J.U.D., The Vow of Poverty, XLIX-217 pp., 1929.
55. Kearney, Rev. Raymond A., A.B., S.T.D., J.C.D., The Principles of Delegation, VII-149 pp., 1929.
56. Conran, Rev. Edward James, A.B., J.C.D., The Interdict, V-163 pp., 1930.
57. O'Neill, Rev. William H., J.C.D., Papal Rescripts of Favor, VII-218 pp., 1930.
58. Bastnagel, Rev. Clement Vincent, J.U.D., The Appointment of Parochial Adjutants and Assistants, XV-257 pp., 1930.
59. Ferry, Rev. William A., A.B., J.C.D., Stole Fees, V-136 pp., 1930.
60. Costello, Rev. John Michael, A.B., J.C.D., Domicile and Quasi-Domicile, VII-201 pp., 1930.
61. Kremer, Rev. Michael Nicholas, A.B., S.T.B., J.C.D., Church Support in the United States, VI-136 pp., 1930.
62. Angulo, Rev. Luis, C.M., J.C.D., Legislation de la Iglesia sobre la intencion en la application de la Santa Misa, VII-104 pp., 1931.

63. Frey, Rev. Wolfgang Norbert, O.S.B., A.B., J.C.D., The Act of Religious Profession, VIII-174 pp., 1931.
64. Roberts, Rev. James Brendan, A.B., J.C.D., The Banns of Marriage, XIV-140 pp., 1931.
65. Ryder, Rev. Raymond Aloysius, A.B., J.C.D., Simony, IX-151 pp., 1931.
66. Campagna, Rev. Angelo, Ph.D., J.U.D., Il Vicario Generale del Vescovo, VII-205 pp., 1931.
67. Cox, Rev. Joseph Godfrey, A.B., J.C.D., The Administration of Seminaries, VI-124 pp., 1931.
68. Gregory, Rev. Donald J., J.U.D., The Pauline Privilege, XV-165 pp., 1931.
69. Donohue, Rev. John F., J.C.D., The Impediment of Crime, VII-110 pp., 1931.
70. Dooley, Rev. Eugene A., O.M.I., J.C.D., Church Law on Sacred Relics, IX-143 pp., 1931.
71. Orth, Rev. Clement Raymond, O.M.C., J.C.D., The Approbation of Religious Institutes, 171 pp., 1931.
72. Pernicone, Rev. Joseph M., A.B., J.C.D., The Ecclesiastical Prohibition of Books, XII-267 pp., 1932.
73. Clinton, Rev. Connell, A.B., J.C.D., The Paschal Precept, IX-108 pp., 1932.
74. Donnelly, Rev. Francis B., A.M., S.T.L., J.C.D., The Diocesan Synod, VIII-125 pp., 1932.
75. Torrente, Rev. Camilo, C.M.F., J.C.D., Las Procesiones Sagradas, V-145 pp., 1932.
76. Murphy, Rev. Edwin J., C.PP.S., J.C.D., Suspension Ex Informata Conscientia, XI-122 pp., 1932.
77. MacKenzie, Rev. Eric F., A.M., S.T.L., J.C.D., The Delict of Heresy in its Commission, Penalization, Absolution, VII-124 pp., 1932.
78. Lyons, Rev. Avitus E., S.T.B., J.C.D., The Collegiate Tribunal of First Instance, XI-147 pp., 1932.
79. Connolly, Rev. Thomas A., J.C.D., Appeals, XI-195 pp., 1932.
80. Sangmeister, Rev. Joseph V., A.B., J.C.D., Force and Fear as Precluding Matrimonial Consent, V-211 pp., 1932.
81. Jaeger, Rev. Leo A., A.B., J.C.D., The Administration of Vacant and Quasi-Vacant Episcopal Sees in the United States, IX-229 pp., 1932.
82. Rimlinger, Rev. Herbert T., J.C.D., Error Invalidating Matrimonial Consent, VII-79 pp., 1932.
83. Barrett, Rev. John D. M., S.S., J.C.D., A Comparative Study of the Third Plenary Council of Baltimore and the Code, IX-221 pp., 1932.
84. Carberry, Rev. John J., Ph.D., S.T.D., J.C.D., The Juridical Form of Marriage, X-177 pp., 1934.
85. Dolan, Rev. John L., A.B., J.C.D., The Defensor Vinculi, XII-157 pp., 1934.

86. Hannan, Rev. Jerome D., A.M., S.T.D., LL.B., J.C.D., The Canon Law of Wills, IX-517 pp., 1934.
87. Lemieux, Rev. Delise A., A.M., J.C.D., The Sentence in Ecclesiastical Procedure, IX-131 pp., 1934.
88. O'Rourke, Rev. James J., A.B., J.C.D., Parish Registers, VII-109 pp., 1934.
89. Timlin, Rev. Bartholomew, O.F.M., A.M., J.C.D., Conditional Matrimonial Consent, X-381 pp., 1934.
90. Wahl, Rev. Francis X., A.B., J.C.D., The Matrimonial Impediments of Consanguinity and Affinity, VI-125 pp., 1934.
91. White, Rev. Robert J., A.B., LL.B., S.T.B., J.C.D., Canonical Ante-Nuptial Promises and the Civil Law, VI-152 pp., 1934.
92. Herrera, Rev. Antonio Parra, O.C.D., J.C.D., Legislacion Ecclesiastica sobra el Ayuno y la Abstinencia, XI-191 pp., 1935.
93. Kennedy, Rev. Edwin J., J.C.D., The Special Matrimonial Process in Cases of Evident Nullity, X-165 pp., 1935.
94. Manning, Rev. John J., A.B., J.C.D., Presumption of Law in Matrimonial Procedure, XI-111 pp., 1935.
95. Moeder, Rev. John M., J.C.D., The Proper Bishop for Ordination and Dimissorial Letters, VII-135 pp., 1935.
96. O'Mara, Rev. William A., A.B., J.C.D., Canonical Causes for Matrimonial Dispensations, IX-155 pp., 1935.
97. Reilly, Rev. Peter, J.C.D., Residence of Pastors, IX-81 pp., 1935.
98. Smith, Rev. Mariner T., O.P., S.T.Lr., J.C.D., The Penal Law for Religious, VII-169 pp., 1935.
99. Whalen, Rev. Donald W., A.M., J.C.D., The Value of Testimonial Evidence in Matrimonial Procedure, XIII-297 pp., 1935.
100. Cleary, Rev. Joseph F., J.C.D., Canonical Limitations on the Alienation of Church Property, VIII-141 pp., 1936.
101. Glynn, Rev. John C., J.C.D., The Promoter of Justice, XX-337 pp., 1936.
102. Brennan, Rev. James H., S.S., M.A., S.T.B., J.C.D., The Simple Convalidation of Marriage, VI-135 pp., 1937.
103. Brunini, Rev. Joseph Bernard, J.C.D., The Clerical Obligations of Canons 139 and 142, X-121 pp., 1937.
104. Connor, Rev. Maurice, A.B., J.C.D., The Administrative Removal of Pastors, VIII-159 pp., 1937.
105. Guilfoyle, Rev. Merlin Joseph, J.C.D., Custom, XI-144 pp., 1937.
106. Hughes, Rev. James Austin, A.B., A.M., J.C.D., Witnesses in Criminal Trials of Clerics, IX-140 pp., 1937.
107. Jansen, Rev. Raymond J., A.B., S.T.L., J.C.D., Canonical Provisions for Catechetical Instruction, VII-153 pp., 1937.
108. Kealy, Rev. John James, A.B., J.C.D., The Introductory Libellus in Church Court Procedure, XI-121 pp., 1937.

109. McManus, Rev. James Edward, C.SS.R., J.C.D., The Administration of Temporal Goods in Religious Institutes, XVI-196 pp., 1937.
110. Moriarty, Rev. Eugene James, J.C.D., Oaths in Ecclesiastical Courts, X-115 pp., 1937.
111. Rainer, Rev. Eligius George, C.SS.R., J.C.D., Suspension of Clerics, XVII-249 pp., 1937.
112. Reilly, Rev. Thomas F., C.SS.R., J.C.D., Visitation of Religious, VI-195 pp., 1938.
113. Moriarity, Rev. Francis E., C.SS.R., J.C.D., The Extraordinary Absolution from Censures, XV-334 pp., 1938.
114. Connolly, Rev. Nicholas P., J.C.D., The Canonical Erection of Parishes, X-132 pp., 1938.
115. Donovan, Rev. James Joseph, J.C.D., The Pastor's Obligation in Prenuptial Investigation, XII-322 pp., 1938.
116. Harrigan, Rev. Robert J., M.A., S.T.B., J.C.D., The Radical Sanation of Invalid Marriages, VIII-208 pp., 1938.
117. Boffa, Rev. Conrad Humbert, J.C.D., Canonical Provisions for Catholic Schools, VII-211 pp., 1939.
118. Parsons, Rev. Anscar John, O.M.Cap., J.C.D., Canonical Elections, XII-236 pp., 1939.
119. Reilly, Rev. Edward Michael, A.B., J.C.D., The General Norms of Dispensation, XII-156 pp., 1939.
120. Ryan, Rev. Gerald Aloysius, A.B., J.C.D., Principles of Episcopal Jurisdiction, XII-172 pp., 1939.
121. Burton, Rev. Francis James, C.S.C., A.B., J.C.D., A Commentary on Canon 1125, X-222 pp., 1940.
122. Miaskiewicz, Rev. Francis Sigismund, J.C.D., Supplied Jurisdiction According to Canon 209, XII-340 pp., 1940.
123. Rice, Rev. Patrick William, A.B., J.C.D., Proof of Death in Prenuptial Investigation, VIII-156 pp., 1940.
124. Anglin, Rev. Thomas Francis, M.S., J.C.D., The Eucharistic Fast, VIII-183 pp., 1941.
125. Coleman, Rev. John Jerome, J.C.D., The Minister of Confirmation, VI-153 pp., 1941.
126. Downs, Rev. Joseph Emmanuel, A.B., J.C.D., The Concept of Clerical Immunity, XI-163 pp., 1941.
127. Esswein, Rev. Anthony Albert, J.C.D., Extrajudicial Penal Powers of Ecclesiastical Superiors, X-144 pp., 1941.
128. Farrell, Rev. Benjamin Francis, M.A., S.T.L., J.C.D., The Rights and Duties of the Local Ordinary Regarding Congregations of Women Religious of Pontifical Approval, V-195 pp., 1941.
129. Feeney, Rev. Thomas John, A.B., S.T.L., J.C.D., Restitutio in Integrum, VI-169 pp., 1941.
130. Findlay, Rev. Stephen William, O.S.B., A.B., J.C.D., Canonical

Norms Governing the Deposition and Degradation of Clerics, XVII-279 pp., 1941.

131. Goodwine, Rev. John, A.B., S.T.L., J.C.D., The Right of the Church to Acquire Property, VIII-119 pp., 1941.
132. Heston, Rev. Edward Louis, C.S.C., Ph.D., S.T.D., J.C.D., The Alienation of Church Property in the United States, XII-222 pp., 1941.
133. Hogan, Rev. James John, A.B., S.T.L., J.C.D., Judicial Advocates and Procurators, XIII-200 pp., 1941.
134. Kealy, Rev. Thomas M., A.B., Litt.B., J.C.D., Dowry of Women Religious, IX-152 pp., 1941.
135. Keene, Rev. Michael James, O.S.B., J.C.D., Religious Ordinaries and Canon 198, V-164 pp., 1942.
136. Kerin, Rev. Charles A., S.S., M.A., S.T.B., J.C.D., The Privation of Christian Burial, XVI-279 pp., 1941.
137. Louis, Rev. William Francis, M.A., J.C.D., Diocesan Archives, X-101 pp., 1941.
138. McDevitt, Rev. Gilbert Joseph, A.B., J.C.D., Legitimacy and Legitimation, X-247 pp., 1941.
139. McDonough, Rev. Thomas Joseph, A.B., J.C.D., Apostolic Administrators, X-217 pp., 1941.
140. Meier, Rev. Carl Anthony, A.B., J.C.D., Penal Administrative Procedure Against Negligent Pastors, XI-240 pp., 1941.
141. Schmidt, Rev. John Rogg, A.B., J.C.D., The Principles of Authentic Interpretation in Canon 17 of the Code of Canon Law, XII-331 pp., 1941.
142. Slafkosky, Rev. Andrew Leonard, A.B., J.C.D., The Canonical Episcopal Visitation of the Diocese, X-197 pp., 1941.
143. Swoboda, Rev. Innocent Robert, O.F.M., J.C.D., Ignorance in Relation to the Imputability of Delicts, IX-271 pp., 1941.
144. Dubé, Rev. Arthur Joseph, A.B., J.C.D., The General Principles for the Reckoning of Time in Canon Law, VIII-299 pp., 1941.
145. McBride, Rev. James T., A.B., J.C.D., Incardination and Excardination of Seculars, XX-585 pp., 1941.
146. Król, Rev. John T., J.C.D., The Defendant in Contentious Trials, XII-207 pp., 1942.
147. Comyns, Rev. Joseph J., C.SS.R., A.B., J.C.D., Papal and Episcopal Administration of Church Property, XIV-155 pp., 1942.
148. Barry, Rev. Garrett Francis, O.M.I., J.C.D., Violation of the Cloister, XII-260 pp., 1942.
149. Bolduc, Rev. Gatien, C.S.V., A.B., S.T.L., J.C.D., Les Études dans les Religions Cléricales, VIII-155 pp., 1942.
150. Boyle, Rev. David John, M.A., J.C.D., The Juridic Effects of Moral Certitude on Pre-Nuptial Guarantees, XII-188 pp., 1942.
151. Canavan, Rev. Walter Joseph, M.A., Litt.D., J.C.D., The Profession of Faith, XII-143 pp., 1942.

152. DESROCHERS, REV. BRUNO, A.B., Ph.L., S.T.B., J.C.D., Le Premier Concile Plénier de Québec et le Code de Droit Canonique, XIV–186 pp., 1942.
153. DILLON, REV. ROBERT EDWARD, A.B., J.C.D., Common Law Marriage, X-148 pp., 1942.
154. DODWELL, REV. EDWARD JOHN, Ph.D., S.T.B., J.C.D., The Time and Place for the Celebration of Marriage, X-156 pp., 1942.
155. DONNELLAN, REV. THOMAS ANDREW, A.B., J.C.D., The Obligation of the Missa pro Populo, VII-131 pp., 1942.
156. ELTZ, REV. LOUIS ANTHONY, A.B., J.C.D., Cooperation in Crime, XII-208 pp., 1942.
157. GASS, REV. SYLVESTER FRANCIS, M.A., J.C.D., Ecclesiastical Pensions, XI-206 pp., 1942.
158. GUINIVEN, REV. JOHN JOSEPH, C.SS.R., J.C.D., The Precept of Hearing Mass, XIV-188 pp., 1942.
159. GULCYNSKI, REV. JOHN THEOPHILUS, J.C.D., The Desecration and Violation of Churches, X-126 pp., 1942.
160. HAMMILL, REV. JOHN LEO, M.A., J.C.D., The Obligations of the Traveler According to Canon 14, VIII-204 pp., 1942.
161. HAYDT, REV. JOHN JOSEPH, A.B., J.C.D., Reserved Benefices, XI-148 pp., 1942.
162. HUSER, REV. ROGER JOHN, O.F.M., A.B., J.C.D., The Crime of Abortion in Canon Law, XII-187 pp., 1942.
163. KEARNEY, REV. FRANCIS PATRICK, A.B., S.T.L., J.C.D., The Principles of Canon 1127, X-162 pp., 1942.
164. LINAHEN, REV. LEO JAMES, S.T.L., J.C.D., De Absolutione Complicis In Peccato Turpi, 114 pp., 1942.
165. MCCLOSKEY, REV. JOSEPH ALOYSIUS, A.B., J.C.D., The Subject of Ecclesiastical Law According to Canon 12, XVII-246 pp., 1942.
166. O'NEILL, REV. FRANCIS JOSEPH, C.SS.R., J.C.D., The Dismissal of Religious in Temporary Vows, XIII-220 pp., 1942.
167. PRINCE, REV. JOHN EDWARD, A.B., S.T.B., J.C.D., The Diocesan Chancellor, X-136 pp., 1942.
168. RIESNER, REV. ALBERT JOSEPH, C.SS.R., J.C.D., Apostates and Fugitives from Religious Institutes, IX-168 pp., 1942.
169. STENGER, REV. JOSEPH BERNARD, J.C.D., The Mortgaging of Church Property, 186 pp., 1942.
170. WALDRON, REV. JOSEPH FRANCIS, A.B., J.C.D., The Minister of Baptism, XII-197 pp., 1942.
171. WILLETT, REV. ROBERT ALBERT, J.C.D., The Probative Value of Documents in Ecclesiastical Trials, X-124 pp., 1942.
172. WOEBER, REV. EDWARD MARTIN, M.A., J.C.D., The Interpellations, XII-161 pp., 1942.
173. BENKO, REV. MATTHEW ALOYSIUS, O.S.B., M.A., J.C.D., The Abbot *Nullius*, XIV-148 pp., 1943.

174. Christ, Rev. Joseph James, M.A., S.T.L., J.C.D., Dispensation from Vindicative Penalties, XIV-285 pp., 1943.

175. Clancy, Rev. Patrick M. J., O.P., A.B., S.T.Lr., J.C.D., The Local Religious Superior, X-229 pp., 1943.

176. Clarke, Rev. Thomas James, J.C.D., Parish Societies, XII-147 pp., 1943.

177. Connolly, Rev. John Patrick, S.T.L., J.C.D., Synodal Examiners and Parish Priest Consultors, X-223 pp., 1943.

178. Drumm, Rev. William Martin, A.B., J.C.D., Hospital Chaplains, XII-175 pp., 1943.

179. Flanagan, Rev. Bernard Joseph, A.B., S.T.L., J.C.D., The Canonical Erection of Religious Houses, X-147 pp., 1943.

180. Kelleher, Rev. Stephen Joseph, A.B., S.T.B., J.C.D., Discussions with Non-Catholics: Canonical Legislation, X-93 pp., 1943.

181. Lewis, Rev. Gordian, C.P., J.C.D., Chapters in Religious Institutes, XII-169 pp., 1943.

182. Marx, Rev. Adolph, J.C.D., The Declaration of Nullity of Marriages Contracted Outside the Church, X-151 pp., 1943.

183. Matulenas, Rev. Raymond Anthony, O.S.B., A.B., J.C.D., Communication, a Source of Privileges, XII-225 pp., 1943.

184. O'Leary, Rev. Charles Gerard, C.SS.R., J.C.D., Religious Dismissed After Perpetual Profession, X-213 pp., 1943.

185. Power, Rev. Cornelius Michael, J.C.D., The Blessing of Cemeteries, XII-231 pp., 1943.

186. Shuhler, Rev. Ralph Vincent, O.S.A., J.C.D., Privileges of Regulars to Absolve and Dispense, XII-195 pp., 1943.

187. Ziolkowski, Rev. Thaddeus Stanislaus, A.B., J.C.D., The Consecration and Blessing of Churches, XII-151 pp., 1943.

188. Heneghan, Rev. John Joseph, S.T.D., J.C.D., The Marriages of Unworthy Catholics: Canons 1065 and 1066, XVI-213 pp., 1944.

189. Carroll, Rev. Coleman Francis, M.A., S.T.L., J.C.L., Charitable Institutions.

190. Ciesluk, Rev. Joseph Edward, Ph.B., S.T.L., J.C.L., National Parishes in the United States.

191. Coburn, Rev. Vincent Paul, A.B., J.C.D., Marriages of Conscience, XII-172 pp., 1944.

192. Connors, Rev. Charles Paul, C.S.Sp., A.B., J.C.D., Extra-Judicial Procurators in the Code of Canon Law, X-94 pp., 1944.

193. Coyle, Rev. Paul Raymond, A.B., J.C.D., Judicial Exceptions, X-142 pp., 1944.

194. Fair, Rev. Bartholomew Francis, A.B., S.T.L., J.C.D., The Impediment of Abduction, XII-122 pp., 1944.

195. Gallagher, Rev. Thomas Raphael, O.P., A.B., S.T.Lr., J.C.D., The Examination of the Qualities of the Ordinand, X-166 pp., 1944.

196. Gannon, Rev. John Mark, S.T.L., J.C.D., The Interstices Required for the Promotion to Orders, XII-100 pp., 1944.

197. GOLDSMITH, REV. J. WILLIAM, B.C.S., S.T.L., J.C.D., The Competence of Church and State over Marriage—Disputed Points, X-128 pp., 1944.
198. GOODWINE, REV. JOSEPH GERARD, A.B., S.T.B., J.C.D., The Reception of Converts, XIV-326 pp., 1944.
199. KOWALSKI, REV. ROMUALD EUGENE, O.F.M., A.B., J.C.D., Sustenance of Religious Houses of Regulars, X-174 pp., 1944.
200. McCOY, REV. ALAN EDWARD, O.F.M., J.C.D., Force and Fear in Relation to Delictual Imputability and Penal Responsibility, XII-160 pp., 1944.
201. McDEVITT, REV. VINCENT JOHN, Ph.B., S.T.L., J.C.L., Perjury.
202. MARTIN, REV. THOMAS OWEN, Ph.D., S.T.D., J.C.D., Adverse Possession, Prescription and Limitation of Actions: The Canonical "Praescriptio," XX-208 pp., 1944.
203. MIKLOSOVIC, REV. PAUL JOHN, A.B., J.C.L., Attempted Marriages and Their Consequent Juridic Effects.
204. MUNDY, REV. THOMAS MAURICE, A.B., S.T.L., J.C.D., The Union of Parishes, X—164 pp., 1944.
205. O'DEA, REV. JOHN COYLE, A.B., J.C.D., The Matrimonial Impediment of Nonage, VIII-126 pp., 1944.
206. OLALIA, REV. ALEXANDER AYSON, S.T.L., J.C.D., A Comparative Study of the Christian Constitution of States and the Constitution of the Philippine Commonwealth, XII—136 pp., 1944.
207. POISSON, REV. PIERRE-MARIE, C.S.C., A.B., Ph.L., Th.L., J.C.L., Droits Patrimoniaux des Maisons et des Églises Religieuses.
208. STADALNIKAS, REV. CASIMIR JOSEPH, M.I.C., J.C.D., Reservation of Censures, X-141 pp., 1944.
209. SULLIVAN, REV. EUGENE HENRY, S.T.L., J.C.D., Proof of the Reception of the Sacraments, X—165 pp., 1944.
210. VAUGHAN, REV. WILLIAM EDWARD, J.C.D., Constitutions for Diocesan Courts, X-210 pp., 1944.
211. PARO, REV. GINO, S.T.D., J.C.L., The Right of Apostolic Legation.
212. BALZER, REV. RALPH FRANCIS, C.P., J.C.D., The Computation of Time in a Canonical Novitiate, X—227 pp., 1945.
213. DOUGHERTY, REV. JOHN WHELAN, A.B., S.T.L., J.C.D., De Inquisitione Speciali, XII—195 pp., 1945.
214. DZIOB, REV. MICHAEL WALTER, J.C.D., The Sacred Congregation for the Oriental Church, XII—181 pp., 1945.
215. EIDENSCHINK, REV. JOHN ALBERT, O.S.B., B.A., J.C.D, The Election of Bishops in the Letters of Pope Gregory the Great, VII—200 pp., 1945.
216. GILL, REV. NICHOLAS, C.P., J.C.D., The Spiritual Prefect in Clerical Religious Houses of Study, X—140 pp., 1945.
217. HYNES, REV. HARRY GERARD, S.T.L., J.C.D., The Privileges of Cardinals, XII-183 pp., 1945.
218. McDEVITT, REV. GERALD VINCENT, S.T.L., J.C.D., The Renunciation of an Ecclesiastical Office, XIV—179 pp., 1945.

219. MANNING, REV. JOSEPH LEROY, J.C.D., The Free Conferral of Offices, VIII—116 pp., 1945.
220. MEYER, REV. LOUIS G., O.S.B., A.B., S.T.B., J.C.D., Alms-Gathering by Religious, XII—163 pp., 1945.
221. O'DONNELL, REV. CLETUS FRANCIS, M.A., J.C.L., The Marriage of Minors, XII—268 pp., 1945.
222. PRUNSKIS, REV. JOSEPH, J.C.D., Comparative Law, Ecclesiastical and Civil, in Lithuanian Concordat, X—161 pp., 1945.
223. SWEENEY, REV. FRANCIS PATRICK, C.SS.R., J.C.D., The Reduction of Clerics to the Lay State, X—199 pp., 1945.
224. VOGELPOHL, REV. HENRY JOHN, J.C.D., The Simple Impediments to Holy Orders, XVI—190 pp., 1945.
225. BROCKHAUS, REV. THOMAS AQUINAS, O.S.B., A.B., J.C.D., Religious who Are Known as *Conversi*, X—127 pp., 1945.
226. GRIESE, REV. N. ORVILLE, S.T.D., J.C.D., The Marriage Contract and the Procreation of Offspring, XVI-224 pp., 1946.
227. BOUDREAUX, REV. WARREN LOUIS, J.C.L., The "*ab acatholicis nati*" of Canon 1099, § 2.
228. BOWE, REV. THOMAS JOSEPH, A.B., J.C.D., Religious Superioresses, VIII-206 pp., 1946.
229. DIEDERICHS, REV. MICHAEL FERDINAND, S.C.J., J.C.D., The Jurisdiction of the Latin Ordinaries over their Oriental Subjects, XIV-153 pp., 1946.
230. DINGMAN, REV. MAURICE JOHN, A.B., S.T.L., J.C.L., The Plaintiff in Contentious Trials.
231. FRISON, REV. BASIL, C.M.F., M.MUS., J.C.D., The Retroactivity of Law, X-221 pp., 1946.
232. GALVIN, REV. WILLIAM ANTHONY, M.A., J.C.D., The Administrative Transfer of Pastors, XII-288 pp., 1946.
233. GORACY, REV. JOSEPH C., J.C.L., The Diriment Matrimonial Impediment of Major Orders.
234. HALE, REV. JOSEPH FRANCIS, M.A., S.T.L., J.C.L., The Pastor of Burial.
235. HENRY, REV. JOSEPH ARTHUR, A.B., J.C.D., The Mass and Holy Communion: Inter-Ritual Law, XII-138 pp., 1946.
236. LINENBERGER, REV. HERBERT, C.PP.S., J.C.L., The False Denunciation of an Innocent Confessor.
237. LOWRY, REV. JAMES MARTIN, A.B., J.C.D., Dispensation from Private Vows, XII-266 pp., 1946.
238. LYNCH, REV. GEORGE EDWARD, A.B., S.T.L., J.C.D., Coadjutors and Auxiliaries of Bishops, X-107 pp., 1947.
239. LYNCH, REV. TIMOTHY, M.S.SS.T., J.C.D., Contracts between Bishops and Religious Congregations, XIV-232 pp., 1946.
240. MCCLUNN, REV. JUSTIN DAVID, A.B., S.T.L., J.C.D., Administrative Recourse, VII-142 pp., 1946.

241. LOHMULLER, REV. MARTIN NICHOLAS, A.B., J.C.D., The Promulgation of Law, XII-140 pp., 1947.
242. McGRATH, REV. JAMES, A.B., J.C.D., The Privilege of the Canon, XII-156 pp., 1946.
243. MARBACH, REV. JOSEPH FRANCIS, A.B., J.C.D., Marriage Legislation for the Catholics of the Oriental Rites in the United States and Canada, XIV-314 pp., 1946.
244. SHIMKUS, REV. BERNARD ALOYIUS, A.B., J.C.L., The Determination and Transfer of Rite.
245. SMITH, REV. VINCENT MICHAEL, A.B., S.T.L., J.C.L., Ignorance Affecting Matrimonial Consent.
246. WACHTRLE, REV. PAUL ANTHONY, A.B., J.C.L., The Baptism of the Children of Non-Catholics.
247. CROTTY, REV. MATTHEW MICHAEL, J.C.L., The Recipient of First Holy Communion.
248. EAGLETON, REV. GEORGE, J.C.L., The Quinquennial Faculties, Formula IV.
249. GIBBONS, REV. MARION LEO, C.M., J.C.L., Domicile of the Wife Unlawfully Separated from Her Husband.
250. KELLY, REV. BERNARD MATTHEW, J.C.L., The Functions Reserved to Pastors.
251. KILCULLEN, REV. THOMAS JOHN, J.C.L., The Collegiate Moral Person as Party Litigant.
252. LAFONTAINE, REV. GERMAIN JOSEPH, W.F., J.C.L., Relations Canoniques entre le Missionaire et Ses Superieurs.
253. LANE, REV. LORAS THOMAS, J.C.L., Matrimonial Procedure in Ordinary Court of Second Instance.
254. LOVER, REV. JAMES FRANCIS, C.Ss.R., J.C.L., The Master of Novices.
255. McNICHOLAS, REV. TIMOTHY JOSEPH, J.C.L., The *Septimae Manus* Witness.
256. MAROSITZ, REV. JOSEPH JOHN, M.S.C., J.C.L., Obligations and Privileges of Religious Promoted to the Episcopal or Cardinalitial Dignities.
257. MURPHY, REV. FRANCIS JOSEPH, J.C.L., Legislative Powers of the Provincial Council.
258. O'BRIEN, REV. ROMAEUS WILLIAM, O.Carm., J.C.L., The Provincial Superior in Religious Orders of Men.
259. PFALLER, REV. BENEDICT AUGUSTINE, O.S.B., J.C.L., The *ipso facto* Effected Dismissal of Religious.
260. POPEK, REV. ALPHONSE SYLVESTER, J.C.L., The Rights and Obligations of Metropolitans.
261. RISTUCCIA, REV. BERNARD JOSEPH, C.M., J.C.L., Quasi-Religious.
262. SONNTAG, REV. NATHANIEL LOUIS, O.F.M.Cap., J.C.L., Censorship of Special Classes of Books.
263. STADLER, REV. JOSEPH NICHOLAS, J.C.L., Frequent Holy Communion.

264. SZAL, REV. IGNATIUS JOSEPH, J.C.L., The Communication of Catholics with Schismatics.
265. WAGNER, REV. URBAN STANLEY, O.F.M.Conv., J.C.L., Parochial Substitute Vicars and Supplying Priests.

www.ingramcontent.com/pod-product-compliance
Lightning Source LLC
LaVergne TN
LVHW050217080826
844660LV00012B/427

* 9 7 8 0 8 1 3 2 2 4 4 0 4 *